History, Mirth and Fantasy

Narrative Poetry and Prose for Romantics and Erudite Dilettantes

By

George Nelson, Jr.

PublishAmerica
Baltimore

ISBN: 1-4241-8189-5
PUBLISHED BY PUBLISHAMERICA, LLLP
www.publishamerica.com
Baltimore

Printed in the United States of America

For Ellen Josephine:

Who endowed me with life, faith in Christ, taught by example and nurtured me;

And Dottie Jean:

Who believed in me despite my foibles and whose unconditional love is the wind beneath my wings that has enriched and sustained me.

Contents

Americana: Heroes, Themes and Places

A New Vision of Classic Entertainment

Heavenly Strains, Cosmology and Spirit Matter

Goodness Will Overcome

The Man in the Mural and Thirty-Two Stars Fallen to Earth

Here in my artist studio I sit,
wondering if I'm spiritually fit
to create something of value and worth
dedicated to the memory of thirty-two stars fallen to earth.
Using color and design brushed on canvas
I desire to represent as best I can—
the infinite realm of imagination,
wherein dwells abundant light and truth.

I feel inspiration
impinging on my conscious mind
to paint a mural illustrating
the conflicting forces raging in the world
between opposing states of good and evil—
of man's inhumanity to man and thirty-two stars,
tragically fallen to earth.

So, I began.
I picked up my pallet,
gathered my brushes and began to paint—
first in earthy tones, then reds, yellows and oranges.
Finally for contrast,
I applied the obscuring pigment of burnt umber.

Now, as I'd finished
I stood back and contemplated
my rendering on the facing wall.
Something seemed diminished
from my original artistic vision.
The execution of strokes and design was superficially good,
however something meaningful and subliminal was missing.

Here in my artist studio
I sit contemplating the work of mortal life.
Should I quit striving for
creative refinement and leave the mural as it is—
an unfinished work of stagnated progress?

All at once it dawned on me.
What was missing was a symbolic representation of the creator—
of his persona and permeating point of view.
It was this unifying creative passion
that never fails to follow through on the little details
that had been missing
from the composition of conflicted beings—
torn between the tyrannical sickness of an evil scheming mind
and the desire for freedom of creative expression
of thirty-two open, aspiring minds.

Yet, I mused,
how can I as the mural's creator
participate with two dimensional images I create?
Can I become one with pigment on the canvas of life
and enter my own illusory world
wholly configured by my
creative will?

The answer came as I painted a renewed center of interest
caused by the impinging rift
of the loss of thirty-two stars on the rise.
The answer was as clear as a ringing bell—
"Yes, you not only can,
but you must become one
with the pigment of life on the canvas depicted."

I hope my meaning isn't too abstruse,
but the Man in the Mural is forthrightly on the loose—
at last escaping the former mural's stagnation
of group and individual's enabling apathy.
The Man in the Mural was now free
to deal prudently with the imposing
specter of those who would rob us of precious life
and conceal themselves silently
in the cast shadows of benighted burnt umber.

At last,
I laid down my pallet and brushes,
and gazed upon my refined rendering contentedly,
if not yet an acclaimed masterpiece as Picasso's *Guernica*—
it was certainly enhanced from the unengaged images previously.

The rendering represented the drama of mortal life
and the human quest for improvement of self,
while also proactively dealing
with the mad impertinent acts of others
through time and continued effort.
This is all that man or God
can ask of any of us.

Here in my artist studio I sit.
I'm finally at peace
and one with the Man in the Mural
who must come to grips with the loss of valued companionship
and the potential gifts of unique merit
of thirty-two stars who were felled before their time.
Sent crashing to earth were they so callously,
by the unfeeling, bestial acts of one
numbered among the unknown ranks of the walking dead.

However, their demise is only momentary,
a birth to a new beginning awaits,
where thirty-two stars shall arise anew,
higher in orbit in the firmament of heaven
and illuminating life brighter than ever before.

Now, all of us are free to pursue our destiny,
under their constellation of undiminished light and truth;
and perhaps, inspired by their radiant luminosity
we will find renewed vigor to oppose the incipient evil of the world
and nurture the collective good in man as best we can.

Such plurality
should not be considered a matter of trivial,
fleeting interest to any of us.
For the bells of freedom yet ring-out unfettered,
across this gracious land of immigrants beginning here,
in this bowed but undeterred Hokie campus family.
They proclaim our mission of enlightenment
and service remains true—
to inspire all men and women to live out their dreams
through positive expression of individual agency
and with profound respect for each other's hallowed liberty.

Yes, with renewed dedication
and animated spirits we each must pledge
to stand with the Virginia Tech family and to persevere,
to carry on, to see this noble mission through...for those fallen,
as well as those who shall follow in the paths
of thirty-two amazing stars
shining brighter than ever in the firmament of heaven.

The Romance
in You

The Cultured Rose
and
Virtues of Love

Whatever the color,
Roses bloom in radiant hues,
Cheerful Yellows:
mirthful, and delightfully fun;
Mischievous Pinks:
hinting at joyful things to come;
Romantic Reds:
expressive of one's true love;
and Virtuous Whites:
rising to lofty ennobling heights.

The rose is singularly gratifying,
unlike any other bloom
in the garden of temporal delights.

In all the bouquet
of life's bounteous wonders,
none is more resplendent,
than the regal princess of flowery
birth!

Straight and free she rises,
from the cultivated earth,
baring buds of petals so politely formed.

Gradually,
the efflorescence of flora occurs,
and opening up the herbal craftsmanship
of nature's intricate design,
she weaves a fragrant magic for all of earth
to breathe in deeply and enjoy.

When singly or a dozen,
nobility is her nature,
a royal heritage all her own.
Grace and femininity does the Rose consistently exude.

Then blows the wind
a gentle whistle,
and while other ladies of Hibiscus,
Petunias, Magnolias or Carnations,
may stoop or squat
in feigned obsequiousness
to the breath of Mother Nature's earth,
the Rose will modestly bend,
with a courtly virtue all her own.

'Tis this elegance of nature
which brings to my mind,
the gayest recollections of
your abundantly flowing warmth and charm.

People are like flowers,
no two being quite identical,
displaying infinite variety in talents, gifts
and other invaluable traits of loveliness.

But,
of all the variants
in the kaleidoscope of life
it has been my pleasure to have known,
none has acquainted me with such generosity of spirit,
and joy in living day to day—save you my darling Dottie,
the cultured Rose of my life,
my companion whose roots enriched the soil of our garden—
as well the worth of my eternal soul!

Gay Blade and His Lady Faire

In a world of learned men,
and neophytes who seldom win,
one is bound to lose,
the sum of hollow pleasures,
to those who can show,
to all the rest the worldly traits,
that indicate,
what pleasure is theirs,
so freely to bestow.

It happens oh so naturally,
or so many have thought,
as a Gay Blade
chatting up his Lady Faire,
the rhetoric of romance would begin to flow,
bringing forth all the love that's in them,
to harvest and to sow.

As often happens in fraternal settings,
several mates stumbled into,
"Gee Bee's" room (as they casually called him)
to cackle and to crow,
"Hey, O' Mighty 'Gee Bee,'
like the narrative of 'Mighty Casey,'
when you came to bat,
we hear a nasty rumor spreading forth
among our fellow Delta Phi's,
that you indeed missed the ball and whiffed,
ingloriously, striking out!
Now, O' Mighty 'Gee Bee,'
we ask ourselves the pertinent question,

why did you venture forth to go,
when for all reality to see,
'Blade,'
you stumbled oh so badly
coming out the starting gate,
that Lady Faire failed to show,
opting for a different bow?"

"Yes 'Gee Bee,'
we think we know the answer.
Even though you're quite disarming,
with your rapier whit so quick,
you beguile most ladies easily,
saying witty phrases like,
'I know Mozart is no Meatloaf,
but come pirouette with me,'
as you deftly glide them across the polished parquet floor,
in graceful, rhythmic dance.
Yes, I marvel at your inherent style and grace—
a truly captivating Don Juan of 'Pas de Deux,'
to Mozart's enchanting minuet!"

"Yet, it behooves us hear your answer.
We fellow chapter members are quite confident,
that even your nimble mind
can not avoid the baited hook
and slither off a second time!"
Hence, united asked they the burning question,
"Who and where, is thy Lady Faire?"

"Well, my brother Delta Phi mates,"
confidently responded Blade,
"I know it must be curiosity that compels you,
to assemble in this venerable hall,
prior to entering my private room,

grilling me with assertive questions,
as if I were a man of dubious reputation,
on public trial,
accused of robbing the Bank of London,
or some other equally nefarious venture!"

"I certainly hope your motives,
have not a nadir's base in jealousy,
for that would not become you,
being far beneath your intimated,
caliber of exalted Cambridge rank!"

"However,
you've made a case so boldly,
and quite eloquently I must add,
that within reason, I feel it appropriate to respond.
Now "Blade" was craftily reeling in his scheming mates
as surely as a game fish on a playing line,
and sensing an opportunity to teach a tale's
morale he continued on…
"Nevertheless, my Lady Faire's
genuine qualities of meekness
and essential goodness do so restrain me,
that I'm reticent to speak much of her
with the flippant likes of you,
lest the art of chivalry be lost to us
and be buried with the other cultured dead
of present-day society."

"Because you've exhibited such passionate interest
in my Lady Faire and our relations to date,
I'll treat the gusto in your queries
with some simple artifices of fact.
No better time exists for me to set you straight—
Just how much more desirous is my Lady Faire,
beyond the ordinary casual date!"

"This past weekend,
of which you so animatedly inquire,
was spent not in idle flirtations.
Rather, we two pleasured in sharing thoughts
on Chaucer, Shakespeare and Milton.
As we renewed our acquaintances
with those lofty English minds,
we also discovered we had much in common
while sharing intimate study of their literate prose and rhyme."

"I can't believe my ears!" snorted Conrad the third,
one disgruntled chapter member. "That you, Blade,
the reincarnated spirit of the mischievous Don Juan,
spent your time in reading while inclined on yonder grassy knoll,
and instead denied yourself the obvious treats
of amorous wooing for two whole days or more?
Me thinks your condition sounds quite serious,
by either impaired health or masculine philosophy,
if you mean you will not bed her,
until arrives the wedding night?"

Taken back for a brief moment
by this effrontery of crudeness,
from one he thought a friend.
He collected his jarring thoughts and replied,
"I'll answer you in calmness,
yet in firmness I declare—
she is the fairest of Ladies Faire.
She is a lady of incomparable talents, warmth and charm—
that she rightly represents to me all that is indeed,
desirable in a wooing lass of 18 to 23."

"Though previously you may have observed me,
in the fleeting romantic embrace of several a dreamy lass,
none does hold a candle's light,
to she who has become my best friend.
Should our joyous relationship naturally mature
into one of abiding love, then united in wedlock,
most faithful lovers we shall always be!"

Thus, having been forthrightly answered,
Conrad the third and several incredulous friends
departed "Gee Bee's" room shaking their heads.
They were left contemplating the unknown essence to them
of the profundity of a committed love's potential
to remarkably enhance and transform.

For those of you
still hoping to be found
by a new love's optimistic glow,
then seek you first a person of substance.
Then astride the walking paths of patience
do not carelessly run.
Rather, stroll arm in arm leisurely
through the flowered gates of kindness and compassion.
Thus proceeding, all the colors of love
will gently distill on you as they did
to a Gay Blade and his Lady Faire
to their eternal benefit.

Have faith and think not that this romantic moral is only true
in realms of dreams, classic fairy tales and late-night movie shows!

The Man with One Eye
Loved Catherine Deneuve

The Man With One Eye
was a top industry executive
whose corporate star was on the rise.
He had a knack for discerning
the minds and intents of people,
of sizing up delicate situations
and reducing the complex
to elements easily manageable.

Yes, the Man With One Eye
was focused always on the objective
and was seldom if ever distracted.
He was uncommonly willful
and acknowledged little,
but that which coincided with his line of thinking.
The rest he casually dismissed
as the flotsam of errant superfluous thought.
Comment on what topic you may,
your perspective was of little consequence to him.
However, should your words
in any way diminish his Freudian ID,
you could safely assume it would rouse his wrath,
and agitate his considerable ire!

Now,
The Man With One Eye
was awaiting notification from the corporate decision makers
regarding his pending election to the board of directors.
His calling and election were all but made sure,
with but one minor test yet for him to pass.

A house party was thus arranged
where the board members and their wives
could be in attendance in order to observe
in a revealing social setting The Man With One Eye.
It was planned that some of the invited guests
would engage The Man With One Eye
in the popular traditional board game of "Clue."
The consensus thinking was,
that if The Man With One Eye
comported himself well
with suitable charm and adequate party etiquette—
the voting for his election would on the morrow be unanimous.

As usual, the night of the party
it mattered not what the subject or activity was,
The Man With One Eye
saw faster than all the rest,
which theory or move was calculated to be the best
to render him a shoe-in to pass this final de rigueur test.

The Man With One Eye,
seemed to others like a wispy shadow on a wall—
an apparition of considerable stealth,
working always on the sly.
Most failed to discern correctly his motive strategy
and could not therefore, foil his astute party play.
So when it suited him, he projected an ambivalent facade
designed to disarm even his most competent competitors
as he observed the game of "Clue" unfold.

However,
The Man With One Eye
watched with contemptuousness
as the player across from him gleefully announced,
"The butler with the wrench in the parlor."
Just like that, it was over and out,
for he who believed himself vastly superior.

Life was a game to him,
a game in which he was all but invincible.
The Man With One Eye felt smug sitting there.
He could lose an occasional roll of the dice now and then,
just to allow his opponents to think that he was vulnerable
before he resolutely squashed them,
for he never lost in the game of life, let alone at "Clue."

It pleased him so to be thus disposed,
as demurely he'd play his hand
rather than by tipping his play
you might become too emotionally comfy.
Other's discomfort was part of the spoils
of his gamesmanship.
It was his way of insuring
you knew not what he was about to do.
Thus he remained composed and in control
behind his mask of calculated deceitfulness.

The options however,
in this particular game were narrowing
with each roll of the die and move of the piece,
because the outcome had been adroitly fixed.
You see, the party givers wanted to observe
what might become of the ample social skills
and legendary composure of The Man With One Eye
if the unexpected happened and he lost.
This could best be accomplished they astutely surmised,
if this occurred in front of so many whom he hoped to impress.

Now, The Man With One Eye thought in his mind,
"Down the hall and into the kitchen,
by Jove, just one more player's turn and this game is mine!"

Then came the planned call
of the rehearsed player preceding him, whose turn it was.
"The maid in the kitchen with the knife,"
said this planted ringer with a broadening smile on his face.
Inconceivable as it was to the Man With One Eye,
he'd just lost a second consecutive game that was his alone to win.
Surely, something was amiss…
or so reckoned The Man With One Eye.

One loss was bad enough
for The Man With One Eye,
but two consecutively was beyond the pale of his reality.
And what's more…all the players seated around
the intimate board parameters
were laughing so very heartily,
were they mocking him?

That was all he could endure
and the studied facade of masterfulness,
began to melt under the heat generated by his inner rage.
Like the wax figure that he resembled,
the streaming beads of molten composure
revealed The Man With One Eye for what he was—
a hollow mannequin devoid of human compassion
and evincing nothing save farcical absurdity.

The Man With One Eye
bubbled over in unameliorated angst
and let fly his considerable temper.
Down crashed his fist upon the game board
with the sound of Maxwell's magic hammer,
and pieces, die and cards,
were all on the fly!

Then murmured his host some moments later,
"With that awesome display of temper,
you can see why the others
made tactful excuses and awkwardly withdrew,
and said what is calculated
and only slightly veiled to be done with you.
I'd safely say you've failed the test
and may assuredly forget election to the board
now or at anytime in the foreseeable future!"

Alienated from his few friends
and the now wizened corporate acquaintances,
The Man With One Eye did not get misty,
nor did he bemoan the blown career opportunity.
That he'd left the party without an explanation or even a goodbye
to his host and former friends was for him not unusual.
He simply disappeared silently out the door
and into the shadows of the night
without an apology or excuses.

The Man With One Eye
shuffled along the sidewalk in the dark of a lonely night,
lost in his thoughts and slowly making his way homeward.
While walking he came upon "The Roxy" —
a retro movie theater he'd often passed before,
but had never entered previously.
The Umbrellas of Cherbourg from '64 was playing.
The Man With One Eye
approached the art deco ticket booth,
purchased one adult admission
and entered the ornate theater devoid of friends.
He sat near the front all alone in the dark,
and began munching buttered corn and sipping pop.

He squinted up with his one good eye
and focused on the lovely face reflected upon the silver screen.
The Man With One Eye thought to himself how groovy it was,
to be alone with Catherine Deneuve,
after midnight, just the two of them,
close together in the dark!

There was nothing to do in lieu of pouting
for the Man With One Eye,
this failed corporate harlequin of magic
who slumped resignedly,
fantasizing of romantic interludes in the dark
and playing the game of "Life" with Catherine Deneuve.

Indeed, he had escaped
the night's earlier disappointments
by fortuitously passing into the romantic fantasies
hidden within the crevices of his nimble mind.
The Man With One Eye
sat passively, but contentedly and imagined
he was romantically speaking words of love
to Catherine Deneuve,
as he embraced her tenderly in the dark!

Heroic Myths and Beguiling Fantasy

Nestor, the Lock Ness Monster

I'm the Lock Ness Monster
and just because I'm a jovial aquatic fellow,
I'll sing you a little ditty that is a favorite of mine:
Oh, I'm the Lock Ness Monster
and Nestor is my name
and reigning royally is my game.
Yeah, down here in the deep, dark, murky abyss,
I cruise in happy bliss,
unstressed by seawalls or wails of whales,
nor any constraints of harrowing seaman's tales.
Yeah, I'm just happy being me,
all alone in this Scottish body of landlocked water,
that is the silent, buoyant Lock Ness to me.

I could swim to far away places,
to visit exotic ports as Madagascar,
if I so in my heart desired.
All I need do is chart my course,
plan carefully the excursion,
then set my gyro and off I'd shoot,
like a runaway torpedo headed for Cairo.
However, here I'm king of the mystic deep,
king of the fishes that abide here with me,
in the gentle currents of peaceful Lock Ness
that I call home, home to me.

Once, I had a hankerin' to troll the seven seas,
perhaps to discover an abode of more promise,
so, I cruised far, far away for many days,
to visit the mysterious, long sought Atlantis.
As it was told by Plato in ancient of times,
one might be received if clever enough,
in the hallowed throne room of his royalty,
the most honorable bat-ray, Sir Mantis.

Before I entered the golden hall, I stammered in awe,
at the glamorous upper crust of Atlantean elite,
all hovering in place to attend his grace,
as if by so doing in some magical way,
this Mediterranean Prince of the Aqua Sea,
might glance to them obsequiously;
thus enhancing their dreams,
having found profound, if fleeting fame,
in his majesty's courtly nod of royal favor.

Gasping aloud at the sight of so many with pride,
finned in their finest ornamental shell regalia,
I quickly turned about with the swish of me flipper,
and I sang Hallelujah, as I swam away.
I've at last found my place in familiar spaces,
however mundane, though it may be.
I'm gladly returnin' to home,
and genuine fishes that I know best,
down in the depths of my ol' Lock Ness
that I call home, home to me.

When I emerged from the secret cavern,
that led to the lock from the frothy endless sea,
I once again scanned the deep,
beneath the waves of comforting home,
and marveled that I was thankfully free…
free of those snooty Atlantean fishes in their
resplendent regalia and their hypocrisy!

As I continued to peer from side to side,
someplace subtly majestic and nearly forgotten,
came into my shimmering view.
Golden green stands of undulating kelp,
that could if needed offer spiritual help,
reaching upwards to astonishing heights,

appearing to be a reverent aquatic cathedral.
Mesmerizing in its silent, gentle trace,
it seemed to me,
an emerald petition of amazing grace.
This was just one among many,
amid other treasures of watery nature,
long overlooked and nearly abandoned by me.
I wondered why…why had I left the best,
these sub-heavenly waters of ol' Lock Ness
that I call home, home to me?

As I joyously swam along,
taking in anew my humble realm,
I noticed the comely shape of a familiar friend.
Why, wouldn't you know, 'twas my ol' girl Myrtle,
the patient and indubitably long suffering deep sea turtle.
"Well, it's good to see you found your way home, Nestor,"
she plaintively bubbled.
Then after pausing and lookin' me over, she added,
"I hope your wisdom, it has been doubled!"

Now, Myrtle and I don't look the same.
I'm long and rubbery,
while Myrtle's quite rounded and firm,
as all can plainly see.
However, I'll bet you,
there'll be no couple happier than we.
You see, I've learned a thing or two
since my carefree swim to Cairo.
You can have all the snootery
of the high finned fishes
that bask in the aura of his royal honor Sir Mantis,
deep down in the golden hall of Atlantis.
I'll take the comforting waters of ol' Lock Ness
that I call home, home to me.

My newfound wisdom whispers to me
like a clam to its pearl:
"Nestor, you'll be far happier
settlin' down in ol' Lock Ness
and marrin' a real fine girl of qualities—
a real true turtle like Myrtle."

Yes, isn't it the truth,
let pass a century from now,
and here we'll still be, doin' our best…
raisin' six firm, rounded turtles,
swimmin' free of the nest,
with long rubbery tales and all the rest,
tryin' with mom and pop to keep abreast,
down in the lovely abyss,
of our cherished home, in ol' Lock Ness
that I call home, home to me.

Saint George:
The Dragon Slayer

Once upon a time,
I went merrily gallivanting,
with Saint George my trusted comrade in arms.
We nobly rode about,
traversing the English countryside
and while joyfully riding,
encountered we,
a most lovely maiden in utter distress and hasty flight,
fleeing the most terrifying and ominous sight.
Said she,
"A yonder fearsome fire breathing dragon,
adorned in colors green and gray,
with thorny skin and bony spikes from head to tail,
sits imperiously across the 'County Squire's Road,'
willfully blocking the way."

It seems
the foreboding dragon forbade any to pass,
without first they pay a toll of pigs or fatted calf.
Unhesitatingly we rode forth,
a noble knight's duty to attend,
to the place where we encountered the insatiable dragon,
just consuming his latest repast.
Gathering my courage,
I challenged him to remove his ample mass,
to one side of the road or the other,
permitting at last,
other stalled travelers to pass on their way,
to hearth and home and anxious families spread
near and far along this country way.

"Not on your life," responded the scornful dragon,
"Now, pay the toll of several pigs or fatted calf,
or turn yourselves around and be on your way,
lest I issue forth my fiery breath,
and molten your armor and melt your bones,
with fervent heat."

"Aye, I'll pay your obnoxious toll you loathsome scoundrel,"
retorted bravely Saint George,
as he drew from his bejeweled scabbard,
his gleaming sword and smote the dragon—
a lightning quick stroke!
His mighty whack fortuitously cleaved
the evil dragon's conceited head in twain.
Lying symmetrically parted in two on the ground,
only harmless smoke now billowed up
where just moments before,
the dragon's fire impeded our way
and held us at bay.

And many another of worthy deeds,
did Saint George and I—his trusted gallivanting friend,
Sir Tristram, do upon other valorous occasions.
So also, did Sir Gawain and Sir Percival,
whom liken to us,
sallied forth in armored combo
with colorful banners,
like kites to the breeze gently floating,
and trumpeter's fanfare triumphantly blowing.

Leaving the confines of protective castle,
mounted on well bred steeds
went we noble knights of Arthurian legend,
to slay recalcitrant dragons,
rescue a lithesome wench or two

and attend to other knightly duties,
until the settling dusk of day
heralded to all—
'tis the hour of retiring for the day.

Thence back across the murky mote,
full of pomp and ceremony rode we
and entered under the towering ramparts,
of loyal nobleman's comforting castle.
After bathing away the grime of dusty roads heroically traveled,
we hastened to celebrate with the gaily costumed maiden's dance.
Next appeared the hilariously performing court jester,
appropriately followed by a bounteous feast and flowing ale,
all a fitting climax to the day's daring deeds.
Then, off to sleep went we to dream
of yet tomorrow's bountiful promise.
Oh, think of it—when on the morrow
Saint George, myself and other joyous knights
shall venture forth to partake anew
of further untold adventures bold!

And so it was,
the fulfilling life of romantic times of yore…
of fiery dragons, of valiant horses,
of courageous knights in shining armor,
of jousting tournaments and colorful pageantry,
of majestic castles,
of noble men and virtuous ladies,
of high ideals and chivalry,
of friendship and loyalty…
as that of the noble Saint George
and his steadfast companion—Sir Tristram—that's me.

The Checkered Flag of Heaven

Somewhere,
up there in the Heavens,
is a ram-shackled old speedway,
awaiting patiently for redemption,
like Gilmore Stadium or Balboa Bowl,
or any one you used to know.

The grandstands are filled to overflowing,
with the animated spirits of those who may be dead,
but you'd never know it by the gleam in their eyes,
or the pulse of their anticipatory chatter.

Down in the infield,
are some of the pioneers of racing:
Fred and Augie Dusenberg, Barney Oldfield, Henry Ford,
Louis Chevrolet, Harry Miller, Fred Offenhauser, and Enzo
Ferrari who were amazingly successful as race car drivers,
engineers, designers, builders, and team owners. Also present
are race promoters and speedway owners Carl Fisher, Earl
Gilmore, Eddie Rickenbacker, Tony Hulman, Bill France Sr.
and J.C. Agajanian among others.

Genius mechanics were still plying their trade,
trying to find something that will afford their driver,
even the slightest, last second edge!

Then comes the call,
"Pit crews, line-up your cars
in neat rows, three by three."
Once that was done,
the starter stood beside each car,
holding his flag aloft as the announcer sang out
each race driver's name,
from now to then and back again.

There were some who'd won the Vanderbilt Cup,
some the great American race—the Daytona 500, some the
"Greatest Spectacle In Racing"—the Indy 500;
and still some who'd raced and won world championships
in Formula One.
There were some who'd won nearly every race they'd run,
no matter the pace,
or how configured was the speedy circuit place.

In Row One,
There was:
1. Ray Harroun, who was first to taste victory at Indy
in the inaugural 1911 race,
driving a yellow and black Marmon Wasp;
and two others who soon followed suit;
2. The handsome Ralph DePalma, who drove his cream,
red and black Mercedes to victory in 1915; &
3. Jimmy Murphy with the luck of the Irish who won
in his Miller powered Duesenberg in 1922!

In Row Two,
There were: Three former Formula 1 World Champions:
4. Twice F-1 World Champ & 1965 Indy Champ—the
diminutive Scottish driver with a lion's heart—Jimmy Clark;
5. Two times F-1 World Champion and 1966 Indy Champ,
the dapper Englishman Graham Hill; &
6. Five times F-1 World Champion, the indomitable racing
Argentinean—Juan Manuel Fangio!

In Row Three,
There were: Three American legends in racing,
each of whom were remarkably 500 Champions
on three separate occasions:
7. The venerated Wilber Shaw in 1937,1939 &1940;
8. The distinguished Louis Meyer in 1928, 1933 & 1936; &
9. The hard-charging Muari Rose in 1941, 1947 & 1948!

In Row Four,
There were: Three NASCAR greats:
10. Glenn "Fireball" Roberts won 24 NASCAR races and was the first to sweep the Daytona 500 and Firecracker 250 in the same season;
11. Lee Petty, a pioneering stock car driver who won three NASCAR Winston Cup championships and a total of 54 races including the first Daytona 500; &
12. Ralph Earnhardt, a racing innovator who won more than 350 NASCAR races during a 23 year career in three divisions and also pioneered driver safety!

In Row Five,
There were: Three European racing masters:
13. Tazio Nuvolari, the Italian who won an amazing 49 Grand Prix races;
14. Alberto Ascari, twice Grand Prix World Champion in his Ferrari; &
15. Rudi Caracciola, Germany's—three times Grand Prix World Champion!

In Row Six,
There were: Two time Indy winners:
16. Tommy Milton, the first to win the 500 twice—he won in 1921 & 1923;
17. Billy Vukovich, the incomparable "Fresno Flash" who won the coveted 500 in 1953 & 1954; &
18. Rodger Ward, two time National and Indy 500 Champ, who drank the winner's milk in 1959 & 1962!

In Row Seven,
There were: Three Indy 500 winners:
19. Bill Holland, the popular and always competitive driver won Indy in 1949 in the famous Blue Crown Special;

20. Johnnie Parsons won in the rain shortened 1950 race in an attractive yellow and silver Kurtis-Kraft; &

21. Jimmy Bryan, a three times National Champ—was the cigar chomping winner at Italy's high banked Monza in 1956 & Indy in 1958!

In Row Eight,
There were: three renowned early Indy winners:

22. Pioneering driver Gaston Chevrolet won in a green and white Monroe in 1920 and reigned regally as Indy Champ;

23. Billy Arnold, the "Hot Shot" chauffeur dominated the "Brickyard" as never before or since by leading 198 of 200 laps to win in style in 1930; &

24. "Wild" Bill Cummings piloted the Miller powered Boyle Special to victory in 1934!

In Row Nine,
There were: Three more Indy Champions of the fifties:

25. Troy Ruttman became the youngest Indy winner ever driving the Agajanian Special to victory in 1952;

26. Pat Flaherty in 1956 piloted his rose and white colored John Zink car to a daring 500 victory! &

27. Sam Hanks, the dignified 500 Champion who upon winning the coveted race in 1957,
pulled into Victory Lane and announced
he was retiring from racing!

In Row Ten,
There were: Three of the most popular American drivers of any era:

28. Tiny Lund, the racing Hawkeye who won a staggering 500 feature events
including the Daytona 500;

29. Tony "The Tinley Express" Bettenhausen, who was twice
National Champion ; &
30. Mark Donohue who was one of the most versatile drivers
ever, winning diverse championships in SCCA TransAm, a
CanAm championship, the 24 Hours of Daytona, and the 1972
Indy 500!

And last but not least,

In Row Eleven,
There were: Three famed open wheel drivers who won cham-
pionships and countless races from coast to coast:
31. Rex Mays, twice National Champion and who was fondly
known as
"The West Coast Terror";
32. Ted Horn, the beloved and respected three times National
Champion; &
33. Jack McGrath, always fast and a perennial favorite
wherever he raced!

Now that the memorable radio voice of the 500 —
Sid Collins,
had introduced the field,
he was followed by Eddie Rickenbaker who uttered a familiar
refrain, "Gentlemen, start your engines!"

Then these thirty three most talented racers pulled down
their goggles while the crews started their engines and pushed
them away,
and around they went on several parade laps,
slowly at first,
waving their hands and calming their wits,
while steadily picking up speed.
Out of the fourth turn they roared,
and over the starting line they sped.

Thirty three former racing champions,
were now competing in Heaven.

The spiritful fans leapt to their feet,
as the starter frantically waved the green flag
for all it was worth.
So it began,
The Greatest Race ever staged.
It simply couldn't be matched,
there'd never been assembled such a field
whether on earth or in Heaven!

What a display of bold driving,
this all-star lineup of crazed chauffeurs
did rapidly put on.
Halfway through this madcap speedway event,
a dozen champion drivers had led the way.
It was still any drivers race to win,
as back markers charged forward
and leaders swapped places at a furious pace.

One hundred laps down,
plus now eighty more,
whizzing around and around,
these bold streaks of color,
made my head spin like Mom's wooden spoon,
churning her favorite cookie dough batter.

Now,
there were fewer than five laps to go,
how frightfully fast they had gone by,
diminishing laps like jaunty magicians,
the thirty-three hurtling racers
made laps magically disappear!

43

Who was going to emerge from the pack,
the anxious crowd wondered?
Who would prove he was better than all the rest,
the "King of Champions,"
whether on dirt or concrete,
he who wins this race,
wins the mantle too,
of the "Big Wheel" who rules the speedway circuits,
in the hallowed heights of Heaven.

As the cars roared around for one final time,
I peered through the mists of time,
racing fumes and celestial dust,
to see who would finally lead down the back stretch.
My heart pounded wildly as I strained to see for sure.
It was a blue and orange "offy" roadster
that appeared to my view—
by gosh, it was ol' number 4.
The inimitable hard chargin' Vuky was leading the pack
as he sailed into three and emerged out of four.
It was my hero Vuky who gunned it for home.
It was Vuky for sure,
way out in front as so often on earth,
he'd done countless times before.
It was my hero Vuky,
who'd brought it home in first once more!

He took the checkered,
which he so richly deserved,
and pulled his victorious mount adorned
with a rabbit and top hat
on the side of ol' number 4,
into a long awaited ethereal winner's circle!

Vuky sat calmly, just breathing it in,
slumped behind the wheel of his ol' number 4.
His work now completed, he'd raced his last race,
for at least a millennium or more.
After swigging some Heavenly milk from a glorious bottle,
he wiped the stardust residue from off his face,
then removed he his helmet, goggles and gloves,
'cause he knew he was finished with them and would need
them no more.
He climbed out of the cockpit of ol' number 4
and for the last time walked away.
There waiting to embrace him were a legion of admirers,
including his parents, wife and family,
all proud as…well, just mighty proud.

When he'd finished with the many hugs and kisses,
he noticed a lone figure standing a few paces away.
Immediately as he turned, he knew it was his grandson Billy the III,
whose mortal life ended in an open wheel racing accident
much like him.
Only, Billy III had crashed in race warm-ups at Bakersfield
and never got the chance to take the green flag, nor motor to victory.
They both had tears in their eyes as they embraced
and then the original Vuky handed the younger,
his weathered helmet, goggles and driving gloves.
With that he turned and pointed to ol' number 4 and said,
"It's all yours now, Billy.
It's your turn to run at the head of the pack,
just like me in ol' number 4."

He'd at last won the race he was leading
several generations and half a century before,
but had failed to finish through no fault of his own.
Fate had stepped in and whisked him away in May of '55,
to save his greatest triumph for a more glorious latter-day!

Yes, it was my hero Vuky,
just like fifty years ago, almost to the day,
who'd shown all the rest the fastest way,
the "Champion of Champions,"
on this Hallowed Race Day!

The Heritage in Historic Places, Cultures and People of Nobility

Joseph and the Pharaoh's Dream

Once upon a time
in the land of Canaan,
lived an aging patriarch named Jacob—
with his wife Sarah and twelve sons.

This tale is one of tribute to the faith and courage
of men who dare to dream
like Joseph,
who wore the "Coat of Many Colors"
in ancient times in the land of Canaan.

Now, this Joseph
who was the eleventh and next to youngest son,
only Benjamin being younger,
was a dreamer of visions—
he dreamed that the sun, the moon,
and eleven stars paid homage to him.

This angered his jealous brothers
to the point, that one day
while out tending their father's sheep in the fields…
they laid hands upon Joseph and conspired to rid themselves
of him.

Their anger was such,
they threw Joseph into a pit and waited…
and then sold they him into bondage,
to a passing caravan
on its way down to Egypt—
to the realm of mighty Pharaoh.

Joseph did not despair,
even though he ended up
in Pharaoh's dingy prison.
Oh, how wondrous
are the unsuspecting ways
and miracles by the hand of Providence.

For God caused Pharaoh
to dream a dream that neither he,
nor any of his wise men could interpret,
and there was great consternation because of this...

They had already searched high and low—
throughout all the realm of mighty Pharaoh
there simply wasn't anyone in the know—
in all the land of Egypt!

Then the butler to Pharaoh
remembered a time he'd briefly met Joseph
while he himself was in prison...
he also recalled that Joseph had rightly
interpreted his own dream—
correctly foretelling of the butler's
return to mighty Pharaoh's good graces.

Thus, he related to Pharaoh
this amazing story
and Pharaoh commanded they bring the Hebrew
to him straight away.
Then they brought forth Joseph
out of prison,
because it was said of him
by the Pharaoh's personal butler,
that he knew Joseph could interpret
the meaning of any dream,
even royal ones that cause such gloom to gather
in both the mind and court of Pharaoh.

And Joseph was bathed
in scented water
and dressed in finest silks
and brought to stand before mighty Pharaoh.
Pharaoh sitting upon his throne,
looked with hopeful expression
and inquired of Joseph,
"Can you give meaning to the symbols
of my dream-vision?"

And Joseph,
by the power of God
gave Pharaoh the answer he sought:
Seven years of bounteous harvest
would be followed by
seven years of drought and famine…
and if Egypt in wisdom
would save the surplus during the former,
Egypt and her people
would not suffer during the latter.

And Pharaoh was so pleased
with Joseph's saying,
that he said, "No more wiser man
than thou,
there be in all my realm.
Thus, I appoint thee, Joseph
to govern the affairs of Egypt
and no man in all the land shall be as powerful as thee,
except it be me."

And with that,
Pharaoh took Joseph's hand
and placed his royal ring upon Joseph's finger,
and placed a golden chain—

as symbol of his power
about his neck.
Now he was esteemed in every Egyptian's eyes
and was known as
Prince Joseph of Egypt,
second in power and authority
only to Pharaoh!

And Prince Joseph went out from Pharaoh
and rode throughout the land of Egypt,
in Pharaoh's second chariot —
which Pharaoh had given him;
and every knee bowed to Prince Joseph
and honored him as a servant of God
and the friend of mighty Pharaoh.

Thus, Joseph ruled the land
of Egypt with compassion and the wisdom of God...
and thankful Pharaoh and his grateful people,
were spared the ravages
of drought and famine.

Hungry, desperate people came to Egypt
seeking grain to sustain their lives.
They came to the land of Pharaoh
from many different places
representing diverse cultures and races,
for there was famine in all lands.

And on one such occasion
came the kin of Joseph —
the eleven famished brothers,
seeking like so many others
to obtain the grain of life...
to sustain their wives, their children,
and even their own aged mother and father.

And Prince Joseph
commanded they be given
all the grain they could carry back
to their families in the land of Canaan.

Prince Joseph at first,
revealed not himself to his brethren...
electing to wait until they returned
to Egypt a second time—
having brought his younger brother Benjamin
from the land of Canaan as Joseph had instructed.

And Prince Joseph was greatly pleased
at the sight of his younger brother
and being reunited with all his brethren.
So pleased was the most high prince of Pharaoh,
that he could no longer restrain himself
and he told them,
"It is I, your long-lost brother Joseph!"

Then Prince Joseph kissed
and embraced them all.
He also told them they need not fear reprisal
for what they did to him many years ago.
He readily forgave them and regardless,
Prince Joseph explained...
it was God's purpose for him
to come down to Egypt
in order that he might fulfill
God's plan to preserve the House of Israel
in a land of milk and honey...
in the realm of mighty Pharaoh,
in the land of Egypt.

And so,
because of Joseph's faith and obedience to the Lord,
Joseph, his father Jacob, his eleven brothers,
their wives and all their posterity,
came to dwell in the land of Goshen,
which was given to them as a new home
by command of Pharaoh.
Here, they made their new home
and over four hundred years
they grew into a large nation
known as the twelve tribes of Israel.

And all of this was accomplished
because a boy who grew to manhood
through adversity in a strange land,
never lost faith in the God he served.
Nor lost he sight of the vision
of his mission that God gave to him
through a young boy's prophetic dream
who dwelt in obscurity in the land of Canaan!

The Pharaoh's Tomb

The First Act
Throne of Glory and Scepter of Power

Surrounded by magistrates,
courtiers and royal princes from afar,
he lived a life of few restraints.
All were servants to this Son of Ra,
a personal butler, a head baker,
they saw to his privy needs.
A sergeant at arms with his royal guard,
marched in unison whenever a need.

As was his custom, Ramses, Son of Ra,
while sitting regally on his golden throne,
summoned his closest aide when ready,
and speaking in barely audible tones,
his royal commands he uttered.

The prime minister's loyal ear having heard,
stepped smartly forward,
and with a wave of his hand,
silenced those who whispered,
adorned in rich apparel of stylish silks, robes and beads.
Without further gesture or courtly command,
all in his presence,
turned in unison to face the Pharaoh seated upon his golden throne
as if controlled,
by a puppet master's deft hand.

Ramses, indeed was descended from Ra,
or so his people were told
and thus, in obedient silence, his subjects stood,
attentive to hear his royal word.
And so it went, day after day,
the Son of Ra's proclamations,
judgments of shrewdness and wisdom,
were followed by forceful declaration:
"So let it be recorded by the royal scribes.
So let it be followed through by the royal magistrates."
And thus it was for all the realm of Egypt ordered
and royal posterity notated.

Then the legion of subjects emptied the hall,
some were contented, others not,
for Ra, nor Ramses, had favored all,
and some forlorn, slunk away,
their courtly entreats not granted on this day.

Many believed the Pharaoh omnipotent.
Thus, did not his armies crush all internal revolts,
or sailed they in ships to distant lands,
where in full battle array they disembarked.
Standing imposingly on foreign soil,
they demanded of foreign kings, princes and potentates —
tribute for Pharaoh in the name of Ra.

Wise were the rulers accounted,
who vacillated not,
sending emissaries and slave carriers laden with treasure
speedily to the commander of Pharaoh's armies.
A king's ransom was paid straight away in gold, rubies and
other precious gems,
fine linen, silks, glorious art, grains, spices and efflorescing plants.

These many priceless things assured temporal grace and saving
peace from the wrath and destruction portended by the presence
of Pharaoh's foreboding army.
All this treasured booty the Pharaoh's army hauled aboard,
stored in vast cargo holds and then heavy laden,
imperiously sailed away.
Upon returning to Alexandria with the substantial tribute of
glittering gold and more, waiting slaves
unloaded the bounteous treasure
as well as the accompanying human cargo of tuneful
musicians, beguiling dancers and artful acrobats—all for the
diversion and amusement of the Son of Ra.

Those few unwise rulers failing to deliver up
the tribute demanded by Pharaoh's commander,
lost not only their kingdom, and riches,
but lost they their heads as well.
Oh, how futile to oppose or resist,
when it meant death, or slavery,
and vast kingdoms broken into bits!

When on those occasions it was required
to slay or otherwise obliterate,
unbowed, unyielding and hostile potentates,
Pharaoh's captain unleashed his armies,
and shortly thereafter,
dead and vanquished was the recalcitrant potentate
who formerly ruled.
Indeed, the dead and vanquished former ruler
was replaced on the barren throne
by command appointment of Pharaoh,
with a sycophant in-law, cousin or favored friend,
that in allegiance to Pharaoh,
would be a loyal soul.

Thus ruled the Pharaoh his sun baked land and far-flung empire.
Decade after decade passed away
with slaves from many lands laboring anonymously,
with heaving breasts, tortured muscles and perspiring brow.
Whipped by ruthless overseers,
and the driven sands of the eternal, restless winds,
they strived on and on with little hope of reprieve.
Toiling countless hours and always short of breath,
they cried to Gods through sleepless nights,
until at last, were they relieved,
ah, by blessed, fortuitous death.
And so it was,
that slaves spent their bondaged lives
raising edifices of heavy stone in tribute to the Son of Ra,
impinging pallid cerulean skies.

Thus the Jubilee City,
was erected to his earthly fame,
pyramids, obelisks and many stone lions
all built to honor his royal name.
Inscriptions engraved on monuments throughout the land,
prominently heralded in literate prose,
his many noble victories of sword,
and dutifully declaring his triumphs over famine and pestilence.
Lastly, was even recounted his subject's pride
in countless beneficial public works,
and eliminating most crime and civil strife.

Soon however,
was approaching his time for departure,
even the Son of Ra, lived not on earth forever.
Careful secret plans were made,
for a cavernous treasure room in which he would be laid.

Then at last,
the time of embarkation arrived.
Not even Ramses,
the Pharaoh—anointed Son of Ra,
could hold at bay the call of death,
and laid he down the golden scepter,
symbol of his mortal power.

Pharaoh's high priests prepared his body,
then in the midst of moonless night,
a chosen few with personal staff and royal guards,
bore off his bejeweled and perfumed body,
to his secret final resting place.
Entombed with untold riches of every kind,
he was accompanied by his servants dead and alive.
Even his royal barge from the Nile,
on which he would embark
upon this eternal voyage through the dark,
was moved, prepared and placed
deep inside the bowels of the towering pyramid.
There, it awaited Ramses in a gloriously
appointed anterior hall,
hidden within one of the many secret chamber walls.

The Second Act
Mindless Voyage into Night

Millenniums passed and Ramses remained,
in utter darkness and silent repose.
Alone he slumbered on, yet entombed in stone,
embalmed in death, wrapped in linen,
and bestowed in regal jewels.
Yet, lifeless he lay encased in wood,
dead and cold, he slumbers long,
long dreary years entombed in stone.

Likewise, the royal barge, made of the hardest woods,
and inlaid with emerald and reflective gold,
rests upon a cradle, forever stabilized and immobile.
It has sailed not a league, nor even one meager meter.
The giant sails of sturdy canvass,
adorned with colorful sunbursts saluting Ra,
remained unfurled, stored in the pitchless hold,
awaiting a captain's command to cast off,
and catch the wind and tide,
enabling her to ride the eternal sea so boldly!

Also there, were many of the artisan's finest works,
statues of gods in marble,
and premier above all—resting on a pedestal
of exquisitively sculpted royal falcons carved of jade,
was the golden bust of Ramses.
In the glimmering image of the Son of Ra
in unexcelled artistry was also depicted the glory of the sun
from whom Ramses was descended.

Also, sitting and lying about as sentinels,
were twenty Nubian oarsmen.
Eternally silent crewmen are they,
destined to labor in seething torment,
a most cruel and tragic seaman's fate.
Now and then,
an apparition appears of black muscled men,
straining to serve eternally,
aboard a motionless ship,
that only rows its oars or dips its bow into,
a ghostly, fathomless, imaginary sea!

Over centuries the tomb remained undiscovered,
the sanctity of Ramses' secret vault undisturbed.
However, its status was about to change.
Some men are always seeking,
not enlightenment or virtue,
rather they lust for that which is hidden
and buried—even forbidden treasures that lay entombed,
just beyond reach, in cold heartless stone.

The Third Act
Pillagers of Antiquity

No one knows for certain,
when the first break-in occurred.
One thing was evident,
these were unscrupulous men,
that came in the dark of night,
with single-minded purpose,
to remove the Son of Ra's icons of status,
the symbols of his power and his light of life.
Robbing the vault of items they could carry,
soon they took their precious artifacts,
then vanished they in stealthy flight.

How many times this pillage was repeated,
is difficult for us today to say.
Clearly, once seals to his vault were broken
and the sanctuary of his remains disturbed,
countless scavengers traversed the musty dark.
Down unlit passageways they crept,
descending narrow steps till last…
they crawled through rough-hewn portals,
uncovering at last the hidden splendor,
of Pharaoh's secret sanctuary and royal tomb.

In time, archeologists discovered,
what previously, only thieves had known,
and when they entered
the hallowed burial chambers of the Son of Ra,
they were struck with awe, as they shined their lamps and saw,
the royal barge, nearly intact, resting on its cradle
as if docked to yonder wall.

When the scholars mounted a ladder,
they carefully peered inside the vessel's hold,
"Yowie!" the first scientist exclaimed.
"We've hit the mother load!"
There in the cavernous hold were all
the artifacts of Egyptian antiquity,
waiting in resplendent repose,
undisturbed, as they were so carefully stored,
millenniums ago.

When the eminent scholars illuminated the anterior hall,
they marveled at the striking murals
that covered all the walls.
While overjoyed by what they saw,
they acknowledged among themselves,
much was missing of artifact treasures
that should have lined the walls.

After taking stock, they queried themselves,
why had the nimble fingered thieves,
bypassed the Pharaoh's royal barge?
Then almost in unison they shouted,
"Look here," "Over there," "There are more by the bow!"
What in haste they'd failed to initially notice in the dim light,
were the scattered remains of the Nubians' bones.
There they lay, silent sentinels in death's repose
waiting for the call that never came to crew the Pharaoh's ship of state.
Within these exalted halls and chambers of deep deathly slumber
awaited they passage from mortality to eternal reward and rest.

Obviously, it was not out of respect,
the thieves feared to board the vessel.
No, it was dread of the royal curse
that caused them pause to tread over
twenty dead Nubians' scattered bones!

With this revelation, the scholars moved on,
with quickened pulse they penetrated
the inner sanctum to Pharaoh's personal vault.
Once inside, they beheld the hand carved sarcophagus,
containing Ramses' mummified remains.
They approached it with trepidation,
not for fear of mortal curse, only heightened expectation
of what artifacts and treasure might be hidden there!

The Fourth Act
The Scholar's Revelation

The exquisite craftsmanship was evident from top to bottom,
with wood inlaid with precious gems,
in colors red and amber,
and Egypt's imperial jade.
Lastly painted was indigo blue,
delineating the finite borders of Ramses' royal sign.

This confirmed,
they adroitly raised the lid,
only to find yet another inner sarcophagus impressively
decorated
by an artisan's crafty hand.
Once again, upon review,
the scholars nodded their consensus,
and proceeded a second time to peer inside;
and examine what was new to them
of unpilfered Egyptian antiquity.

This time most agreeably,
they'd found a treasure trove
of long lost royal artifacts within!
There Ramses lay,
a Son of Ra from ancient days,
a golden scepter placed within
the mummy's lifeless hand.

There was yet a greater find—
the greatest prize of all.
It was Pharaoh's royal necklace,
lying regally on his wrapped breast,
with many strands of precious gemstones.
At once it was so beautiful and sparkling,
they could not speak and only gasped.

Surely the best had been miraculously withheld from
the benighted scavengers as well as even these latter-day
seekers of truth,
until all had been at the very least,
properly humbled!

These archeological scholars made copious notes
and photos to remind,
where every single artifact was found.
Even pottery shards were noted and cataloged
and soon will be on display with others from antiquity.
Nothing must go uncollected or be abandoned once again,
to the dusty halls of memories,
or capricious fates of time.

Once again it's dark within the royal mummy's haunt.
All the artifacts, including Ramses' himself,
were packed and sealed and delivered rightly,
for further study and display
to the famous National Museum of Cairo.
Where else but this learned institution,
could mummies, jewels, pottery shards and golden scepters,
possibly go and still end up uniformly on display?

Not withstanding all the men,
both learned scholars and daring thieves,
who eventually found through secret doors
and passageways within—
the royal treasures of the Pharaoh's hidden tomb,
there is still a timeless moral of far more lasting value,
for those, who instead of grasping ancient baubles,
took the time to look within.

By the time his sarcophagus was opened
the plasma of Pharaoh's life had long since ceased to flow.
Now I wonder as he dwells in spirit prison
with legions of other benighted souls—
who lived only to gratify their personal ambitions and appetites,
does he ever wish he'd taken the time to adorn his eternal soul,
with acts of kindness and varied fruits of charity,
that do not canker or despoil?

Those Nubians, whose bones lay scattered in the dust,
amid the compost lying there,
does not a better fate await them
than does the judgment awaiting haughty, mighty Pharaoh.
For they and others who served Pharaoh,
were sons and daughters adored by loving parents too,
who would not exchange one reunited embrace with them,
for all of Ramses' wealth,
nor even the impotent golden scepter
that once symbolized his power and royalty, yet no longer!

Epilogue
Charity Adorns the Eternal Soul

Simply queried,
in common rhetoric,
how great is Pharaoh now?
What is it he does possess inherently,
that reckons him a prince among
the innumerable spirits of dead men
held universally in the unremitting grip of purgatory's specter?
His once sacred earthly sanctum pierced and bare,
is now little more than a robber's lair,
where once his cherished artifacts piously lay,
have all been callously swept away,
by shadowy men of stealth.

None during Ramses' life,
sought Pharaoh more earnestly than these lowly, hungry men,
whom dead gods were impotent to hold at bay.
Yet common purpose had they each at heart,
those who from him sought courtly favors
or those who came centuries later through the dust of and
muck of time,
to rob and be off on ostentatious lark!

If only they and Pharaoh had known
this one enduring truth,
that in the realms of angels and heavenly hosts on high,
only those who possess nobility of virtue
and a scarcity of pride reign virtuously supreme.

Only ones with charity in their hearts
and love unfeigned toward their fellow man,
who serve in gentle meekness
and obey our Lord's abiding will,

lay up in store in heaven,
like the bread that was leaven,
and assure themselves eternal life
among the host of heaven.

Unlike poor Ramses
or the filthy men who stole his treasures,
learn this simple truth while yet you breath…
rob not thyself of virtue,
for that which lives immortally,
resides somewhere within each person's eternal soul,
and by the grace of Christ our Lord,
is truly pillage free!

Conquistador's Dream

The Passion of Conquest

Oh Conquistador,
Ye noble Spanish hidalgo,
how many leagues have ye traveled
in wooden ships under sail,
with unbounded dreams
of fame and fortune to acquire.

The wind in the sails
propels the galleon carrying ye
from old world to new,
following the stars of ancient constellations.
Across uncharted seas come ye,
with the dreams of many an adventurous mariner—
seeking undiscovered treasures
awaiting a courageous hand
to claim for the Crown of Spain,
dominions of bounteous lands.

New World Adventures

Oh Conquistador,
America's untamed lands
and indigenous wealth
beckon ye…
ye who are clad in sun glint armor;
riding forth with flags unfurled
fluttering in the freshening breeze
the colorful pennants of Charles V,
his royal majesty.

How imposing a visage are ye,
nobly astride equestrian steed,
ye boldly lead
a column of armed, lusty men
marching and riding forth
with jeweled swords held high
and silver shields emblazoned
with the scarlet cross
and emblems of Castilian pride…

Following along the dusty trek with ye,
comes the humble,
yet resolute Franciscan Father,
grasping a worn bible
in one hand,
and holding onto his trusty staff
adorned with wooden cross,
symbol of the Son of God,
in the other.

Off ye went
toward adventurous destiny
with dreams of discovery…
of lost civilizations,
of cities of gold,
of confronting vast native armies
festooned in feathers and puma skins,
armed with spears, bows and arrows.

Metal Clad Men

Among these benighted savages
the brave Conquistador that once ye were,
would charge,
leading thy metal clad men

in hewing them down
with every sword stroke and musket shot—
till the native warriors
fainting from loss of blood
and paralyzing fear...
surrendered themselves up to ye...
as well their city,
and all their hidden treasures of silver and gold.

Destruction of Indigenous Gods and Culture

Once the battle ended,
the men of the cloth
observing stone idols of Indian worship,
ordered them destroyed by cannon blast...
and so ye were compelled to act,
reducing feathered serpent symbols
of Quetzalcoatl and jaguar gods
to shattered, unrepentant fragments
of stone strewn in disastrous heaps.

And that was not enough,
for the Franciscans also demanded
all hints of idolatry be erased,
and foot soldiers set about
destroying every vestige of indigenous culture:
their false gods, native art and codexes—
tracing royal lineages and historic genealogies,
burning their bibliotheca of priceless ephemeral
treasures to the ground;
and up in smoke went all the traces of native origins,
from whence they sprang and how they came to be
in this new world of discovery.

The Dreams of Gold and Glory

The Conquistador's dream
was always the same.
It always ended with
the faith of Christ
implanted in the minds of vanquished
native souls…not always by choice,
but also out of Indian's fear
of being drawn and quartered.
And more ye dreamed—of finding vast stores
of gold and silver artifacts,
of returning triumphant
to the Spanish harbor of Valladolid,
with galleons laden with unimaginable treasures
of exotic description and untold wealth,
to present to his majesty.
Then in turn, you would be awarded
grants to lands and titles
as Adelantado de Florida,
or perhaps something as regal
as Viceroy de Nueva Espana
by the appreciative pleasure of his majesty.

All Points of the Compass

Oh Conquistador,
off ye went exploring
in every direction from Cuba's Santiago and Havana,
with Juan Ponce de Leon claiming La Florida
for Spain in 1513, while searching for
the fabled Fountain of Youth—that life giving spring
that renders old men young and virile again.

Ye searched in vain until de Leon
was mortally wounded by Indians,
losing his life in the attempt to conquer mortality.

Then, with Hernan Cortes and 600 men,
ye sailed from Cuba in 1519.
Eventually landing at a suitable spot he named Vera Cruz,
ye marched onward gathering allies
of resentful, subdued native tribes.
For they hated the Aztec reign of tyranny
and eagerly joined themselves to ye,
perceiving Cortes as the long rumored white and bearded savior.
United, Cortes with his indigenous allies
attacked the Aztec capital of Tenochtitlan.
There, after many hazardous battles
and suffering through the infamous "Noche Triste,"
Cortes and his combined armies defeated the imperious
Moctezuma
and destroyed the beautiful island city of Tenochtitlan,
that grew wondrously like a multi-hued lily pad on the lake.
Then further westward ye sallied forth to establish the Pacific
port of Navidad.

And again,
with the ever wandering Cabeza de Vaca,
ye endured eight years of harrowing adventures
and hardships while traversing 6,000 miles of the North
American continent.
Embarking from Northern Florida in 1529
and hugging the Gulf shores to a calamitous landing near
Galveston Island,
where the expedition floundered.
Years of frustrating delays, defections
and illness led at last to de Vaca

and three weary compatriots trekking successfully at last to
Nueva Espana in 1536,
having discovered the mouth of the mighty Mississippi River
along the way.

There was no end to the lustful search for gold
and conquering native chieftain's far flung empires.
So, with Francisco Pizarro ye ventured forth seeking easy wealth
as he conquered the vast South American empire of the Incas
and put to death their emperor Atahualpa
of Peru in 1532.

A few years later
occurred the incredible Homeric odyssey of Hernando De Soto,
who landed near present-day Tampa Bay after departing Havana.
Seeking a Peruvian like cache of golden treasure,
he boldly led his men exploring northward
and then Southwestward
through the interiors of today's states of Florida,
Georgia, the Carolinas, Alabama, Arkansas and Mississippi.
After fighting off Indians and starvation much of the daunting way,
the intrepid leader fell ill and passed away.
There, ye buried the brave De Soto in a watery grave
beneath the rushing waters of the Mississippi;
and all of this occurred along the wanderer's way
from 1539-43.

Not to be outdone by previous bold captains from Castile,
Francisco Vasquez de Coronado,
being inspired by native stories of golden cities to the Northeast,
sallied forth with an army of adventurers from Compostela in
Nueva Espana
in search of the fabled seven cities of gold in the magical land
called Quivira.

Finding nothing but poor, destitute Indians,
he trooped his armed adventurers from Cibola
through the Pueblo Indian lands and ultimately all the way
into the distant plains of the Kansas territory and back again.
From 1540-42 ye searched fruitlessly with him
until ye were compelled to return empty handed
and in disgrace to Nueva Espana.

Oh Conquistador,
all over the New World
ye searched mostly in vain,
for few found that for which they searched—
as the Fountain of Youth
or the Seven Golden Cities of Quivira.

Nefarious Greed and Plunder

Was it worth the price
that dream ye dreamed
that compelled ye onward?
That unrelenting beat of drums
in thy single-minded head,
like the beat of thy heart were the incessant,
pervading drums that compelled ye:
drums of conquest and conversion,
drums of trinkets—gold and silver,
drums of lands and slaves to work them,
drums of heraldry and honor,
drums of glory and splendor,
drums of mighty conflict, frightful death
and eternal slumber…

Epilogue

If only ye had sought to sow the golden verities
that rise from noble dignity and honor,
and truly been emissaries of our Lord's merciful saving grace—
think of what ye might have reaped.
Alas, no amount of benighted native's gold
can compensate for lost generations of indigenous peoples
and the eternal splendor of celestial brotherhood
ye might've enjoyed…
had ye only been motivated by more than nefarious
greed and plunder.
Oh the sorrowful waste and wonder!

People of the Promise:
The Death of Tecun Uman

The Story of Prince Tecun:
My Name Is Tecun:

That is what my family and close friends call me.
Everyone else addresses me as Prince Uman or Tecun Uman.
This they do because of my family's exalted status.
My father you see, is King of the Maya,
and rules his people moderately
from his golden throne,
in his "Palace of Jade"
in the royal city of Copan.

I want to tell you our story,
but there isn't much time left to me,
or space on these gold tablets
to inscribe the events of our people's tragedy.
The invaders from across the sea
and their allies from the north,
after last night's bloody battle,
are in determined pursuit of me
and the remnants of my eagle knight led,
jaguar clad army.

Also, I'm making this record on two plates of gold,
which is all I have left after ceasing from flight,
momentarily to rest, record my thoughts,
and consider what action is best for those left of us.
Thus, here is the record I make while yet I live:

The Record on Plates of Gold

Behold, I am Prince Tecun Uman,
the first born of my father,
heir to his throne, his kingdom,
and leader of his valiant Jaguar armies.

I have received a message of blessing,
from our High Priest of Quetzalcoatl.
Before tomorrow's rising sun,
illuminates the murals of inner temple walls,
our high priest will in solemn ritual tonight,
offer sacrifice to the majestic green Quetzalcoatl bird,
symbol of our god and master.
He will supplicate the feathered serpent god,
Quetzalcoatl, that he deliver us from imminent disaster.

Murals on Temple Walls

Always before, from my earliest memory,
on certain days of the year
selected by the chief astronomer,
the animating warmth of the rising sun
bathed the mural pigments with life.
The aged high priest and the wizened astronomer,
would often bid me to sit on a folded blanket,
facing one or another of their meaningful murals.
As the illumination subtly shifted,
in changing angles of dancing light,
upon the murals some figures faded into darkness,
while others inevitably ascended
from obscurity into the prominence
of the illuminating day.

I learned from my two special mentors,
regarding the royally appointed artist and the master builder,
had designed together that both rooms and murals,
would thus in tandem function harmoniously.
Like an author and allied performer,
they sketched a play within a painted scene,
and in degrees of luminosity according to the time of day
the characters played out upon a mural wall—
the scenes of typical Mayan life.
Thus the pigmented narratives served as both guide
and similitude of temporal and spiritual life.
They fortuitously foretold significant dates of the cyclical codexes,
portending the future of every Mayan life from royal king,
to rural farmer and even other animate things!

The high priest promised Ximche Uman,
my honored father,
that the colorful murals contained the secrets,
to providential Mayan life.
Hence, reading them correctly,
while performing required priestly rituals,
constituted his covenant with Quetzalcoatl.
The Feathered Serpent God of Quetzalcoatl
always understood our Mayan people's needs.
We were assured by the high priest,
that Quetzalcoatl would provide needed rain for crops,
a bounteous harvest of life sustaining maize,
and victory over every threatening foe,
thus glorifying Quetzalcoatl's emerald reign.

A Prince's Recollection

Ironic, how on the eve of a desperate battle
that will decide the fate of my people,
I sit here with thoughts of long ago.
How clearly I recall my adventuress youth,
my father's wise reign,
and the remarkable history of my intelligent,
industrious Mayan people.

They excelled in math, architecture, and the arts.
So also were they masters in building
broad causeways to massive temples,
rising high over flowering gardens,
flowing fountains, sculptured stella,
majestic courtyards and regally adorned palaces,
of well planned and meticulously designed Mayan cities.

Mayan astronomers comprehended
the cosmology of times and seasons
and observed and dutifully recorded celestial wonders—
of myriad stars and planets that twinkled,
whirled about, around, and like comets,
raced through the multiplicity of orbs,
abounding in ethereal heavens!

The discoveries of our diligent astronomers
were always recorded as harbingers of things to come,
many times beneficial and on other occasions
potentially disastrous.
Such significant celestial events,
were by our God Quetzalcoatl predestined,
to affect the Maya and our rigid cultural structure,
which reflected life in our highly devoted world
of consecrated order!

What happened this time, who erred,
that there was no prophetic utterance,
by the Feathered Serpent's priests, cosmologists,
or the maize of life's respected agronomists?
It was a meaningless query.
Nothing more could have been done,
save what brave hearts envision
and unfailingly step forward to do—
confronting incipient evil with resolve,
as brave men with brave hearts inexorably do!

These unsettling thoughts wrenched me,
back to the present context…

I repose in my tent with my loyal captains,
awaiting a runner with word from my father.
We desire to know the royal city of Copan's status,
the current disposition of enemy forces
and if any warriors,
the city's defenders can spare us.

Tomorrow, before the haze of afternoon,
it will be finished.
The acts of death and battle,
will have consumed a part or all of us.
Either they or we will stand victorious,
and if by decree of Quetzalcoatl, it be us,
then, shall we live to fight again
at another time and place,
until there no longer lives in our lands
one bearded, white-skinned invader.
Nor, any of his sycophant Tlaxcalans.

When all our enemies are dead
and their remains are dispersed
by the winds of Quetzalcoatl into oblivion,
then will we rejoice and do the feathered serpent dance
of Quetzalcoatl anew!

The Eve of Battle

In several hours,
long before the first light of day,
we will attack with all our might,
hoping to catch the enemy by surprise,
falling on them and reeking havoc.
Before the men of iron can mount their beasts,
and gain tactical advantage over us,
we must visit them with merciless slaughter!

Our scouts report they are camped,
in the jungle of Huey Huey Tenango,
just outside the Mayan community of Zaculeu.
In strength, they are several hundred men less than us,
one thousand warriors full of fight have we.
We fight to preserve our land, our families,
our way of life, and our sacred feathered serpent god,
Quetzalcoatl, who from the sky, watches over us.

On the other hand, they are driven by greed,
lusting for the mineral the color of maize.
They come to put asunder all we hold dear,
to unearth precious minerals, and bury us!
Oh, please, sacred Quetzalcoatl,
please, we reverently supplicate to thee,
let them not succeed in destroying us!

Now it is time to give my captains the word,
to wake and organize my jaguar clad army,
to have them eat a last meal.
This, they do in order that they be fortified with energy,
for the march in darkness to the place where we'll encounter
the enemy
and engage them in ferocious, mortal struggle.

Battle at Zaculeu

Two hours later,
following rapid though stealthy march,
we arrived at the place of the enemies' encampment.
It was just as described to us by our reliable scouts.
We wasted no time encircling them,
and when all my men were in place,
I gave the signal and the carnage of battle did begin!

Though we contested valiantly by moonlight,
attacking our enemy's camp while they slept,
and early on carried the fight,
slaying naked men and riderless beasts alike,
still we did not prevail.

We were on the precipice of victory,
when out of the dark, without warning,
we were attacked on our flanks
by fifty mounted men in armor
and four hundred mercenary Tlaxcalans.
They had joined the foreigner's ranks,
based on promises of sharing the spoils of war.

The battle raged anew,
as we struggled to turn and face,
this deadly new threat.

The men of steel rode upon four legged snorting beasts!
Rearing-up, they charged my courageous warriors,
trampling many of them under their hoofs in the dark.
We lost several score men before we could react!

Valor of the Eagle Knights

With valor though, my bold captains,
known to us as Eagle Knights,
rallied our jaguar clad warriors just as it seemed
our hard fought advantage might be lost
and counterattacked,
even more ferociously than we had the first.
We dealt death to the Tlaxcalans,
with ever thrust of spear,
every flight of arrow,
our enemies' numbers were lesser.
And numerous enemies fell by the bash,
of the potent obsidian mallet!

Now, with our fiery surge,
deep holes we hacked in their ranks,
slaying more than one hundred Tlaxcalans.
Nor did the mounted invaders of riding beasts,
escape our fury.
But we were tiring too,
from our wounds,
loss of blood and strenuous pace,
of protracted killing.
As soon as we could,
we disengaged the enemy,
and by the grace of Quetzalcoatl,
we in order, strategically withdrew.

The Tragic Aftermath

We had won a tactical battle,
putting to the spear, arrow and mallet,
more than twice the slain as we had suffered.
Yet, it was a hollow, empirical victory,
as we learned through the night and into the morning,
following our strategic retreat.

Additional fresh reserves of forces,
keep flowing unto them from the north,
from conquered Tenochtitlan
and various allied tribes that originally,
came together with the Men of Iron
and their wrathful bearded leader—Cortez!
As did the dishonorable Tlaxcalans,
who, in vanquishing the reviled Mochtezuma,
and subduing his tyrannical Aztec empire,
bartered away their future for promises of treasure.

Now I've learned from several captured Tlaxcalans,
that these beguiling alien invaders,
have flattered other tribal leaders of the north,
to send warriors to join in the conquest,
of not only our noble Maya,
but all the other unsuspecting tribes
in the far lands to the south of us,
who will soon be in peril as well.

News from Copan

Now the morning rays lighten sky and earth.
What portends the dawning day?
In the distance far…we can observe on the horizon,
several dark plumes of smoke,

searching the heights of azure sky.
Are they signaling the likelihood,
that our people have perished through the frightful night,
one and all having met their tragic fate,
in the royal city of Copan?
I wonder, if you can possibly feel,
the terrible anguish within my soul,
having to contend with my people's inglorious end.
Yes, impotent to aid even my own family and kin,
all of whom are scurrying to escape
the deathly plague of insidiously evil men!

Copan was the stronghold of my father,
the capitol of all the present Mayan lands,
of the mountains, of the jungles and the high plateau!
Fearing for my family's welfare…I pondered,
which route would afford us,
quickest and safest passage
from our present location,
a day's fast march to the royal city of Copan,
to my father's aid upon his golden throne.

Just as I was pondering,
a royal messenger at last had found us,
announcing the unwanted, disheartening news
of the fall of our beloved royal city,
and annihilation of its lovely gardens,
majestic temples and the ornate palaces of Copan,
that were famous in all the Mayan world,
for their colorfully rendered facades.

Although the king's forces were marshaled,
and well prepared as ever before,
King Uman's courageous eagle knights and jaguar warriors,
could not contend with the alien invader's fearsome weapons:

like an active volcano,
they boomed a terrifying noise as they erupted,
spewing forth smoke and flame,
and flung spheres in mercurial flight,
till upon landing they burst with awesome force,
and broke into a hundred pieces,
whatever object was their misfortune to have struck!

Heritage of the Ancients

No, the royal city of Copan was doomed,
the nobles, priests and others with their families,
were fleeing by predetermined plan,
to the remote northeastern jungle wilderness,
to where our ancient fathers first came to dwell anciently
after disembarking from a perilous ocean journey
according to our ancient mythologies;
and over time, built they a rich and glorious civilization,
unsurpassed by that of any people to be found on earth.

Those revered ancient ancestors
and each succeeding generation
carefully bequeathed to the next,
both written records and oral traditions
of that most sacred time.
Included in these was the most sacred story
of when the Holy Son of Quetzalcoatl,
flew through the vaulted heavens,
and descended unto them!

The blessed Son of our God Quetzalcoatle,
taught them enlightened principles of truth,
and gave to them sacred rituals,
to keep them in remembrance of solemn covenants

and their special lineage to him,
who is the divine creator,
of the heavens and the earth!

The Plan of Escape

Now, the royal messenger after catching his breath,
related the rest of my father's message,
that I should take my men and haste,
to a predetermined remote mountain pass.
This pass is the only known entrance
from this direction of our high plateau,
that provides access to the near impenetrable jungles
where in the midst of was located
our ancient ancestor's place of first abode.

Along the way I was to gather in what straggler's I could,
that were fleeing the carnage of ruined Copan.
I was determined to safely escort them to the prudent pass,
where what remained of our forlorn people,
Should be nestled in.

With my heart aching,
and my eyes swollen red by caustic tears,
I cried out, "Oh sorrowful soul,
behold, how the many creatures flee
and my Mayan people's blood runs in rivulets
down to the sea.
The royal Quetzal bird has taken flight,
surely, it's an ominous omen that bodes ill
for our Mayan people's fearful plight!"
Yet, I must gather myself and my faltering emotions,
For there is still time to preserve a remnant of my people
in order to fulfill the destiny of our fate.

Five Days Later

We'd lost some men in running skirmishes,
along the long and grueling way.
Still, we had for the most part,
fulfilled my father's last command—
in saving from tortuous death or slavery,
as many of our frightened, forlorn people,
as our strength, time and providence did permit.

Now, as my surviving captains
gathered to my side,
we peered from our mountain summit
upon at once a majestic and imposing scene.
We observed a vast expanse of verdant unknown jungle,
that none of us save two had previously seen.

We knew at once,
it would require all our collective courage,
and the precious few resources
that some had providentially brought along,
in harried flight of preservation,
from the fall of Copan,
and the death of Mayan civilization.

It was unanimously decided among us,
numbering approximately thirty-five hundred,
that all our resources would be held in common,
in order that each soul might have the best chance to survive.

That night nearly all of us but a few who kept watch,
slept a death like sleep from sheer exhaustion,
and fortuitously we did not dream.
Nor did we conjure apparitions of missing loved ones,
or horrific scenes of conquest we might have seen!

In the years ahead there would exist,
ample time for grieving,
if indeed any survived the arduous task of relocating,
deep in the daunting, foreboding jungle.
We sought a safe haven of tranquility,
from where we could begin,
to test our collective inherent mettle,
and build our lives again.

As did our long departed progenitors,
who, so the legend goes,
arrived from far, far away, across the deep wide ocean,
to make for themselves a new life in a promised land
of milk and honey—that was free of tyranny.

None of our priests survived the battle for Copan,
or in resulting chaos managed to escape
to come and join us here.
I regret this sad, sad outcome,
as we have no one to bless us here.

I remember though the words
of the wise old high priest,
who regularly took opportunity to admonish me,
from my youth to present day.
"Never embark on any great endeavor,
unless, first you see to make a worthy sacrifice,
in the formally prescribed, traditional way,
as you have here to for been repeatedly instructed.
And while kneeling in obeisance before the fiery altar,
forget not to utter in the privacy of your mind,
and the sanctity of your soul,
a word or two of humble supplication
to Quetzalcoatl, the God of all creation,
and the Son who flew through heaven,

to bless this land "Bounteous,"
just as did our ancient parents,
that it might become a tamed and hospitable abode,
and no longer a hostile wilderness unto us!"

So, I summoned my people together,
and shared my heart with them,
and lamented the loss of our old wise high priest,
that we had no official one in his high office,
to bless our way this day.
Yet, if they would kneel before me,
I would in faith to the Feathered Serpent,
symbol of our God who flew through the heavens,
and descended from the sky,
offer a worthy sacrifice and make obeisance to him,
and recite these words of prayer,
the Holy Spirit has graciously revealed to me this day.

All our assembled host knelt down in unison,
closed their eyes and listened reverently,
to hear the spoken word.

The Humble Prayer

"Oh God of all creation, Dear Quetzalcoatl,
hear the words on behalf of your people,
I speak to you this day.
Now we have the choice
in this same verdant realm,
as did our honorable first parents,
and call in fervent supplication,
to the Son of our God, Quetzalcoatl,
that he might manifest himself to us,
or our children's children in a latter-day.

Thus we hope that we too may be blessed to behold his holy person,
as is the promise to all whose blood is of Israel,
and receive of him, wisdom and eternal blessings
as did they, many centuries ago,
in this once adopted land by strangers,
then mysteriously abandoned and forgotten,
this choice land blessed above all others,
this eternal promised land!"

The Exodus

Once I had finished they silently arose,
and while still gazing upon me in tenderness,
I gave my final instructions and expressed
my genuine affection for them…
and then came the most difficult thing,
I've ever had to do.
I bid farewell to them, explaining…
a few of us single men would remain behind,
to act as a rear guard, to protect the pass,
and to insure they would not be followed.

I once again assured them,
that we would surely join them in just a day or two.
Then at last, I bid them to please be on their way
and I stood and watched as if I were a sentry at attention.
This beloved remnant of my proud people,
less twelve of my closest friends who stayed
to guard the pass with me,
wound down the mountainside and finally
disappeared into the verdant,
tangled growth of the remote jungle.

They had become an invisible, lost remnant,
of a once proud and noble people,
who had fallen and no longer existed,
to the knowledge of the world.
I prayed they would remain so
until the time was right,
and they had matured in wisdom
and risen in obedience,
through the graciousness of our Lord of Light.
The Holy Spirit whispers to me they will surely be revealed
to you anew in future times—a glorious, godly tribe of
people,
like the proverbial city on a hill!

Epilogue

Nothing was ever heard from Prince Tecun Uman again,
or any of the twelve disciples who remained behind
in order that these loyal friends might spend
their remaining mortal hours together
and guarding the way.
They remained inseparable,
as they had been all through life,
even so, valiant brothers until the very end!

Several days later,
the remnant people under the leadership
of the man who was a favorite of Tecun,
and appointed second in command,
tarried at a base camp before preceding deeper,
and sent two runners back to find Tecun and his men.
They returned to report, that there was no trace of Tecun or his men.
There was no evidence of combat or any sign of pursuing armies,
or any threatening thing.

There was just one single item discovered
lodged between two rocks,
where our noble Prince Tecun Uman was lastly sighted,
standing so erect and saluting us,
until he faded from our sight.

The precious object we found,
was a shallow wooden box with Tecun's initials on the top.
Inside it contained two tiny golden tablets,
fashioned like metallic pages—thin yet durable.
Upon both Tecun had inscribed the events in sequence,
of this past heart rending week.
But that which was most dear to us,
and we will always keep implanted in our hearts,
no matter where we journey or what our fate may hold,
was a poem he had composed for us.
Undoubtedly, he had inscribed it
during his last remaining hour.
The poem spoke of faith, love and everlasting hope!
And this is how it read:

My Beloved Maya People

How dearly, dearly I will miss you,
until we meet again in Heaven,
where the Son has prepared a place for us,
a place of everlasting joy
where families are eternally together,
bound by boundless love
and the Royal Priestly Power
of the Only Begotten of The Father.

He, who flew through the heavens
and descended unto us full of Truth and Grace
and gave unto our fathers in this promised land,

principles of light and truth
and his own Holy power
to administrate his kingdom for a time…
Then, there shall come a falling away
wherein the people shall dwindle in darkness,
until the time of refreshing
when cometh a restoration of all things
as declared by all the Holy prophets since the beginning.

In that latter-day shall be fulfilled all the promises
that God has made to man through our ancient patriarch
Abraham;
and all the House of Israel will be gathered
from the distant isles and hidden places of the earth,
and even the Lost Tribes of Israel shall be revealed in the
north countries,
and their prophets shall lead them to a New Jerusalem
to be blessed by the hand of Joseph.

Not long thereafter,
when sounds the holy angel's trump,
then comes the Son of Man a second time,
the Prince of Peace and King of Kings,
this time in power and great glory,
to receive his footstool back again!

I testify in his Holy name,
Jesus The Christ
That every word is true—oh seek ye after him!

Until we are blessed to meet again, and we will,
for thus the Son of God has promised me,
I bid you love and fond farewell.
In Jesus Holy name,
Amen, and Amen.

Tecun Uman

Native Nations

Now,
gather round the campfire
and listen to the elders
tell of our tribal fathers,
and of their historic fight.

It's a daring tale of courage
and nobility of purpose,
to preserve our sacred earth—
our burial grounds wherein the spirits
of our departed ancestors do dwell.

Carefully listen now,
as too, I will tell you
of our once abundant hunting grounds
that teamed with indigenous life—
the forests, the rivers,
the mighty mountains and their gurgling streams,
the eagle, bear and cougar,
the fishes, deer and beaver,
and of course the majestic herds of buffalo
roaming free like inland whales
through vast flowing seas
of prairie grass upon the eternal plains.

Once upon a time,
all of this America belonged to us
many moons and sorrowful seasons ago…
to all the tribes of North America:
the Mohawk, Huron, Seneca, and Iroquois,
the Shawnee, Cherokee, Choctaw and Seminole,
the Chickasaw, Potawatomi, Kickapoo and Dakota,
the Sioux, Pawnee, Osage and Cheyenne,

the Apache, Kiowa, Arapaho and Comanche,
the Blackfoot, Crow, Ute and Shoshone,
the Pima, Hopi, Pueblo and Navajo,
the Nez Perce, Paiute, and Mojave,
the Chumash, Modoc, Yakima
and Chinook…
and many others,
did this vast natural wealth
of Mother Earth belong.

Our Indian peoples
lived, hunted, harvested
and rode…
all across this native homeland
until the white-man came.
Then of necessity,
the tribal councils convened
and after much meditation
and supplication to the Great Spirit,
our many chiefs of many tribes did meet in council.
The chiefs at last,
decided to take up the tomahawk, bow and arrows,
adorn themselves in war paint
and resist the white-man's imperious encroachment
of our native lands.

We followed our brave chiefs,
among whom were:
Tecumseh, Pontiac, Geronimo, Crazy Horse and Sitting Bull.
Bravely in both war and peace did we strive with the white-man,
but alas, nothing worked.
Always more came of them
with their frontier forts and booming guns,
with their iron horses and talking wires,
and with their ever expanding settlements
until we were overwhelmed.

Then,
the white-man's government men came
with treaties in extended hands.
We were offered peace, tribal lands and sustenance by them,
if we would but cease our raids
and agree to live in peace
on designated lands called Indian reservations.

The reservation
became a dead end destination to many of us,
who've long since returned to spirit.
Life on the reservation
was where old men withered unto death
and young braves became as squaws,
no longer in possession of a fighting spirit.
The reservation was no more than a prison without walls
from which there was no escape,
and many a brave sought solace
in non-fulfilling bottles of spiritual poison
called alcohol.

However,
be assured my Native American brothers,
our tears and sorrows will fade into distant memories
like feathery clouds
riding fast upon the prairie winds.
Someday, not too far distant,
just beyond the painted sunset,
the Creator of Mother Earth
will stretch forth his hand again,
to reestablish us from our long banishment.
If you listen attentively,
you may hear the Great Spirit's voice softly in the gentle breeze,
calling us home to our sacred lands,
where once again we'll be
a mighty, cultured and noble people!

He'll renew the earth
and heal her spirit...that all of us
who in the past were dispossessed,
may regain our historic tribal lands,
set aside our long-held animosities,
and live in everlasting harmony with each other
and hopefully too, our repentant white-skinned brother.

The Romance in Britain

I am the unembodied,
collective spirit of Great Britain.
Can you sense the romance in me?
How many tales of classic chivalry,
from Arthur Pendragon to Sir Lancelot,
have played out upon a parent's knee?
Wondrous stories of fantasy and myth,
noble deeds and mighty steeds,
they all make up a part of me.

Abide with me for a brief spell and I shall account
but several of our mythic tales and history.

Robin Hood and King Richard

Oh brave Robin,
protector of maid Marian,
share with me an intimate glimpse,
of arrows flight and clashing swords,
of those who fight courageously
to restore our beloved King Richard,
our most noble sovereign,
from the grasp of nefarious Leopold,
who holds King Lion for ransom,
in Austrian prison!

While here at home in troubled England,
Norman barons levied oppressive taxes,
upon humbled impoverished Saxons.
And the king's own brother,
the conspiring Prince John
aided by his lustful Norman barons,
sought to usurp,
his brother's rightful throne.

Robin with his loyal Sherwood men,
intervened in the nick of time,
outsmarted the scheming Prince John
and saved for Richard his royal throne.
Throughout the realm united Saxons and honest Normans alike—
good men and true cried,
"Banish the evil Prince John,
that ignoble charlatan,
from Lion Heart's true realm,
forever more!"

Chaucer's Canterbury

The literate prose of Chaucer,
with abundant wit and charm
brought to life the Elizabethan era,
through many engrossing and revealing tales
of Canterbury's courtly intrigues.
I must admit a delicious fascination for Chaucer.
As imbibing the wine of dandelions
and dallying with the ladies faire,
would hold a certain fanciful attraction
for one of his courtly characters.
However mischievously appealing it seems to be,
I must regrettably proceed to weightier matters
of national destiny.

Shakespeare's King Henry V

One of my proudest recollections,
that outshone many memorable events,
was the challenge to us on the plains of Avignon,
while riding with our noble sovereign King Henry V.
As the inimitable William Shakespeare in sublime prose related,

we were opposed by the French king
and many a knighted noblemen,
arrayed against us in vastly superior numbers.
I solemnly pledged with my brothers there—
on St. Crispin's Day,
our valor and fealty to England and her monarch,
we would display.

And when the clarion call to battle sounded,
the haughty French charged in all their multitudes,
bowmen, swordsmen and knights in shining armor,
advanced on our strategic position,
all the while in tumultuous shout,
clamoring as they charged,
to spill our life giving "sangre."
Yet nay, it was not us so much as they,
who fell to earth with mortal wounds,
failing to taste the sweets of valored victory
this remarkable St. Crispin's day!

Alfred Lord Tennyson
and the Charge of the Light Brigade

With Sir Alfred's pen in mind,
I charged with the six hundred,
attacking the dastardly guns.
Through smoke filled hell we rode,
to the sound of enemy cannons
and lastly reaching their fortified lines,
over them we leaped,
dealing death by well aimed lance
saber stroke and pistol shot!

Then rode we back,
what was left of us,
dreadfully shocked and nary a one not wounded,
straggling back were gallant scores of men and horse,
several hundred noble survivors!

But not all,
for many a gallant British lancer,
who moments before,
charged pell-mell in righteous fervor,
now, with their obedient mounts lay strewn,
broken and forlorn on Crimea's tortured battleground,
abandoned by capricious fate.

No, not nearly all returned,
of the valiant six hundred—
our fury and blood expended
on the charge of Balaklava's heights.
By genius or blunder ordered,
what does it matter now?
For all the Russians stared in awe and marveled,
"How courageous they be," said they,
"these daredevil men on horseback,
who charged in courageous, brilliant maneuver!"

From Crimea to the China Sea
and many ports of call across the bounding main,
my sailors in their mighty sailing ships
have kept the oceans safe and free for centuries.
Lord Nelson and the admiralty assure me confidently,
that as the Spanish armada of the empire seeking Prince Phillip,
was sunk and dispatched to the English Channel abyss,
thus, It shall always be to any foe who threatens tyranny.
And thus filled are the pages of our Royal Naval history.

Der Fuehrer's Plan

Centuries later,
there came again, a mustachioed tyrant,
bent on destruction,
of all men's God given liberty.
In *Mien Kampf* he wrote of his evil thoughts,
a perverted hegemony he sought,
not by will of the people
expressed at the ballot box;
but rather in the black of night.
In secret gatherings of like minded devilish souls,
these co-conspirators plotted in secret oath,
to intimidate, murder and thus subvert,
their fatherland's duly elected government.

And pulled it down, piece by piece
through conspiracy and stealth,
indeed these nefarious conspirators did!
Then with corrupted power in their lustful hands,
they drank a toast to Der Fuehrer,
in the blood of the hapless innocents,
and tragically—not a very few.
The Nazis consolidated their power via intimidation and
horrific holocaust,
robbing the lives of six million Jews!

Now, all of this once beautiful land,
from the Rhineland and
its fertile valleys to the hinterland,
including Berlin and all of Prussia too,
was coalesced in benighted power
by blackened hearts in blackened men,

that marched in mechanized armies,
by tens of thousands,
in perfect goose-stepping unison declaring aloud,
the Treaty of Versailles was dead.

First they struck their unsuspecting neighbors,
imposing their will initially in Austria and then Czechoslovakia.
The Nazis then unleashed their mechanized armor
racing through Poland—causing Britain and France
to reluctantly declare war with Germany.
Yet, the Nazi mechanized forces moved so swiftly,
the allied democracies of Britain and France were powerless
to aid the Poles to halt their rapid advance.
Sorrowfully, the Nazi's lightning blitzkrieg
ultimately reduced much of beautiful Warsaw to rubble
and induced the government to concede.

The same was true in lovely Copenhagen, Denmark;
as one by one capital cities and nations fell: Oslo, Norway;
Rotterdam, Netherlands; and Brussels, Belgium too.

The Maginot Line in France was then swiftly defeated.
The capital landmarks of once romantic Paris,
the Eiffel Tower and Parisian boulevards along the Seine,
lost their luster in the darkening gloom of Third Reich occupation!

Nearly every city and town,
all across the European continent,
of formerly independent nation states,
now reeled under the blackened hand of Nazi tyranny and hate!

With all this accomplished and as well the fall of France,
the dreaded Panzer Meister turned to Great Britain,
now atop his invasion list.
Der Fuehrer ordered Goering to send his iron eagles—

those Messerschmidt and Heinkel combat airplanes
winging in, laden with bombs — hell-bent on destruction.
Through all the tumult and the horror,
as the ravages of unmitigated air war raged
across the English Channel,
Britain, the mighty lion stood firm,
yet alone,
to defend the world's liberty.
Now the might of Goering's aerial armada,
threatened to bomb into rubble the Isle of Wight
and all of Brittany!

The Battle of Britain

"Scramble A flight!"
went out the call to intercept the airborne Huns,
who in force with Heinkel bombers
and escorting Me-109s were flying in to the attack.

Strapped in,
canopy closed and goggles on,
I poured the power on.
Racing over the squadron's grassy field,
I hear no cough or sputter of my Spitfire's straining engine —
only my lusty Merlin's powerful roar.
Scrambling skyward in my trusty Spit,
flying high above the clouds
and the patchwork quilt of country farms,
we Royal Air Force pilots in formation rise to the deadly challenge.

"Below us at five o'clock,"
our flight leader cries.
"Tally Ho! Attack and break them up!"
We dive to intercept the Nazi cross,
emblazoned on the German planes.

Rolling over and over in fearsome flight
we aeronautically tumble.
Then, out I climb triumphantly only moments later,
while vanquished Hun spins in missing a wing,
his aeroplane riddled with bullet holes and all in flames
trailing a blackened plume of smoke,
an Me-109 meets its fiery end!

In soaring exultation,
over the White Cliffs of Dover,
I fling my climbing Spit into a victory roll,
high above the British clover!

And many a Brit still echoes to this day,
Sir Churchill's lofty praises,
"Never has so much,
been owed by so many,
to so few."
Hail to our valiant Battle of Britain airmen,
who triumphed over Hitler's best—
the unflagging ground crews and the bold pilot aces
of our spirited RAF.

Summary

Noble knights from mythic legends of King Arthur's Camelot,
to stirring tales of courageous Sir Galahad
and his endless quest for the "Holy Grail,"
and other stirring yarns of chivalrous deeds by noble knights
and royal kings;
and more significantly was the precedent setting history—
of English barons who compelled King John
to seal the Magna Charta at Runnymede.

Then, we must recall Wellington's stirring victory
over Napoleon at Waterloo,
and from Flanders's tragic fields to the heroic Battles of WWII.
I, the collective spirit of Great Britain wonder—could the
world perceive,
that all these epic adventures and historic calamities
make up a part of me.
I wonder, oh, I wonder,
could they ever fathom the profundity in me?

Noble, Noble Great Britain

Oh Britain,
glorious Britain,
may you always be,
a proud ensign of the truth,
yielding not to slovenly entreats,
and
may the hosts of heaven always declare:
"Thou blessed isle and worthy people,
together joined thou doest comprise noble, noble Great Britain.
Thou art the Royal Lion of the Sea, the Land and of the Air;
and in thy historic realm doest repose all the dreams of
faithful hearts,
that live to beat,
into the choicest realms of eternity!"

Remembering
World War Two

The Wisdom Owl of China

Memories of a Glass Sculpture and a Girl Named Tanya

A little over a year ago, at my wife's urging, I had decided to either sell or throw away the collected ephemera of decades of waxing and waning interests in the multiplicity of things—mostly pop-culture items produced by our eclectic society. Our basement, according to my wife, resembled a museum's abandoned collection of artifacts, carelessly stored in a dusty, forgotten warehouse.

Continuing she said, "It was as if some old curator had once intended this 'stuff' for an exposition on 20th century popular culture and had become indifferent to the idea or simply too forgetful to remember where it was stored."

That was Dottie's subtle way of suggesting it was time to reduce my "collection" to a more manageable volume. She preferred that I open the more than one hundred deteriorating boxes and determine which of the contents were really worth saving—if any. Then after disposing of the non essential items, I could catalog and neatly repack what was left. In her mind, that was not to exceed fifty percent of the original "stuff" into new durable storage containers.

As I began the tedious process of searching through the mountains of dilapidated boxes I quickly realized it was I, she had been referring to in her analogy of the absent minded curator. I had forgotten that I had actually saved about a third of the materials so far uncovered, and of the remainder, maybe twenty percent escaped me as to what original purpose I had determined to retain them. However, having said that, I did discover a number of things that brought back fond memories of people, places and times long ago.

The Wisdom Owl of China

One such object, was a most unusual aquamarine colored glass statuette/pitcher in the shape of a perched owl. I had given this unusual object to my mother as a birthday gift over thirty years ago. Not uncharacteristically, she adored it because of the special sentiment and history inherent in it. Over the years, she had kept the translucent fowl prominently on display in her china cabinet. Whenever any of Mom's friends would inquire about the lovely and distinctly attractive Owl she would take the time to patiently relate the remarkable history of the glass art piece.

That was my mom! She was more interesting and unique than anyone I can think of, other than my wife Dottie, who closely resembles her in personality and character. Mom was very sentimental and was touched by the unique story of the artist who created the owl as well as the family who graciously sent it as a special gift for my mom on the occasion of her sixtieth birthday.

When Mom passed away several years ago, this was one item of hers that I wanted to keep for sentimental reasons. Yet, in the end, I decided my mom's memory wasn't going to fade, so why keep this glass icon of our close relationship, especially as we were short of either display or storage space.

As I affectionately held it in my hands, turning it around, studying its charming glass details, my mind drifted back over the decades to how and where I had initially discovered the aqua colored glass bird...

The year was 1955. It was mid-June. I was still in a somber mood from two weeks earlier when my childhood hero—race car driver Billy Vukovich—had died in an auto racing crash while trying to win his third consecutive Indy 500! There was no one like the "Fresno Flash." I had watched him win one of his biggest races right here at the market speedway (Gilmore Stadium) five years ago on "Turkey Night."

He always seemed to be able to drive his midget racer closer to the edge than any other driver. Maybe that is why I and legions of other Vuky fans were so attracted to him. His life of daring do, touched the "Walter Mitty" in all of us.

Nowadays, especially since Vuky's demise, I have few illusions about life. Everything seems to lack a quality of permanence. We all realize that life is fleeting, yet we all hope to find that certain something we can believe in beyond mortality, that makes all of this temporal foolishness appear rational and meaningful.

"El Segundo"

I am an average screenwriter (very average) on assignment with one of the minor motion picture studios (very minor) in town. The studio head, Thornton Shields II, had (so the story goes) inherited a sizeable portion of his father's Oklahoma wildcatter oil wealth and promptly decided to relocate to Southern California to find his own success.

Dreams, like those of Mr. Shields II can be heady, magical stuff, and it doesn't hurt to have several hundred million dollars of family money to pave the way toward success. Yet, money alone doesn't guarantee it. After securing financing, the challenge of recruiting talented, honest and dedicated personnel is the most important factor for achieving corporate goals.

That is where Mr. Shields has an Achilles heel to date. He bought some land in the City of Industry that he planned to develop as the site of his motion picture studios. The property had roughly twenty acres of dilapidated warehouses in an unappealing, blighted industrial area southeast of downtown Los Angeles. The acquisition was consummated at the insistence of his general manager, who had accompanied him from Oklahoma.

First lesson, don't employ or even listen to business advice from friends. Slightly over three years later, the property is still in litigation, has consumed one tenth of Mr. Shields' available assets and is not a spade of dirt closer to becoming a movie studio.

Thank goodness for that! Who in his right mind would have wanted to be employed in a creative endeavor such as film making, in such a culturally deprived wasteland of crime and pollution. The wayward GM was subsequently dumped unceremoniously and he retreated to Oklahoma a year ago. Mr. Shields has in the interim, leased a portion of a moderate but viable old studio in Hollywood in which to begin his dream of becoming a successful producer of motion pictures.

The Assignment

My job was to create story concepts, synopses and treatments for consideration of development for production. Mr. Shields or "El Segundo" (the second one) as I referred to him privately, seemed to like my offbeat writing style. He liked the classic film noir genre of the thirties and forties, especially the films featuring Bob Mitchum or Humphrey Bogart.

Consequently, I was assigned the task of coming up with an atmospheric story similar in feel, pace and plot to the Maltese Falcon, which was a big hit in 1941 for Warner Bros. It also just happened to be "El Segundo's" "primero" movie favorite.

Mr. Shields wanted something on paper, at least a synopsis with a projected initial budget not to exceed $1 million which was an austere production, even for 1954; and he wanted it within one week in his hot hand! "No problem," I confidently blurted out in response, as he left my office. Yeah sure, no problem, except I was sure I was brain dead. It was Monday again, and I hadn't had a decent new concept enter my mind in nearly two weeks.

Shields wanted the story set in a contemporary setting in order to keep production cost from soaring. I needed to get out of my sterile office environment and seek some inspiration for the story's setting—somewhere rich in a milieu of colors, textures and sounds and conducive to the imagination process. Another random thought entered my mind, I had not yet purchased a gift for Mom's birthday which was only five days off.

Kapow! It hit me like a runaway Lionel Train on Christmas morning: Farmers' Market! I decided in a micro second to eat lunch out at the venerable marketplace at Third and Fairfax and kill two "birds" with one stone, so to speak. Anyway, our studio lacked a functioning commissary—only a lunch wagon that arrived on the lot each day about noon. For all intents and purposes, we ate out every day.

Crossroads of the World

Ah, Farmers' Market, located in the southwestern corner of Hollywood, it was about as exotic and colorful a setting as one could hope to find. Even in quirky California it was unique. That's why locals referred to the outdoor marketplace, bazaar and entertainment center as the "Crossroads of the World." It was indeed frequented by all types: Hollywood celebrities, wannabe celebrities, foreign visitors from all around the world and Midwesterners hoping to catch a glimpse of Cary Grant or Doris Day shopping or eating lunch.

Knott's Berry Farm it wasn't, however, it was real. It consisted of independent merchants that leased booths and stores where vendors marketed fresh meats, poultry, fish, vegetables, fruits and nuts of every kind. You could buy fresh juice drinks of every flavor. Soda shoppes offered ice cream in a myriad of flavors and exotic concoctions such as date shakes (with fresh dates from the palm groves of Indio Valley).

There were several pastry and donut shops, and candy vendors where you could watch as every confectionary imaginable was made fresh daily from hand pulled taffy to chocolate coated apricots; and full service restaurants including the venerable Dupar's, famous for its homemade soups, pies and buttermilk pancakes.

My favorite food spot was the Western Pit Bar-B-Q, where I routinely treated myself to the best BBQ pork or beef sandwiches ever. Whatever your pallet desired, you could find it at the Market. If you couldn't, you probably wouldn't want to eat it anyway.

The same was true with the non food vendors. Every kind of

merchandise imaginable was available: imported toys, men's and women's specialty apparel, jewelry, arts and crafts, luggage, furniture, newsstands, book stores and pet shops.

If all of this wasn't enough, when you were done eating or shopping, the Market offered plenty of leisure-time diversions as well. And they were all conveniently located within a pleasant stroll from each other on the Market grounds. Gilmore Stadium hosted special events of all kinds, but was most famous for its weekly midget racing events that were well attended by celebrities including race fans Clark Gable and Mickey Rooney. It also occasionally hosted high school, college or semi-pro football games.

Also, once you'd placed that last shopping item in the back seat, you could go directly to Gilmore's Drive-In Movie theater without leaving the parking lot. Lastly, there was Gilmore Field. The attractive wooden ballpark was the home of the Hollywood Stars minor league baseball club.

The Ball Game

That's where I was headed first. Gilmore Field—the Hollywood Stars were playing a double header today against their arch rivals, the Los Angeles Angels. The Angels featured the "Big Bopper," Steve Bilko.

Bilko was their main attraction—a large physical specimen who played first base gracefully and routinely drove the pelota (ball) out of whichever ballpark he happened to be performing in. The Angels were promoting this season as "The Year of Bilko!" This was to be the season the "Big Bopper" would break the "Babe's" record of sixty round trippers in a single season. He came close last year with a total of 55 homers.

I took my regular seat behind the home team dugout along the third base line where I could maintain an ongoing support banter with the "Stars." Indeed, I also enjoyed looking for an opening or some sort of weakness in the "Angels" I might exploit verbally.

I had a firm grip on my dog. The last time I "lunched" here, an overzealous fan while exuberantly reaching for a pop foul ball, knocked my dog from my grasp and into my Coke! The thought of another mustard flavored Coke was not my idea of a mixed drink.

Before I knew it, the game had progressed to the top of the ninth inning. Nearly three hours had passed by since I'd parked my '49 Ford Woody Wagon in the lot north of the market and adjacent to the entrance to the ballpark.

The game had been knotted at 2-2 since the fourth inning. Then came the top of the ninth and our old nemesis, "Big Bopper" Bilko. He was slated to hit sixth in the inning, so I wasn't too concerned that the Stars wouldn't get out of the inning before he even came to bat. So far, our pitcher had done an admirable job keeping him and their other hitters in check. Wayne Lumpky had gone all the way for the Stars while only giving up one earned run. Lumpky had mesmerized the opposing batters with his tantalizing variety of off-speed pitches: curves, change-ups, sinkers, and his "floater" that flew like a drunk sailor trying to navigate his way from a San Pedro bar to a waiting taxi at 1 a.m. Lumpky didn't have a strait pitch in his entire repertoire.

The Stars' manager decided he had lived on the edge as long as he dared with Lumpke and replaced him for the top of the ninth with the team's ace closer, "flame throwing" Del Vaughn Rey. It was a sound decision as far as baseball strategy goes. The hard throwing Rey, also known as "The Phenom" would be quite a contrast for the Angels after watching Lumpky's junk pitches for eight innings.

Rey, a nineteen-year-old lefthander with an extremely live arm, had been signed directly out of Glendale Hoover High School the previous year. He was a late bloomer with loads of untapped talent. He hoped to develop his skills with the Stars in the Pacific Coast League and then be picked up by a major league team.

Rey started off the ninth in fine fashion, striking out the first batter on three fastballs. He quickly jumped ahead of the second batter in the same fashion with two high hard ones that overpowered the hitter's feeble attempts to swing and connect. On his next delivery, Rey fooled the Angel hitter by coming with the heat again, only down and away. Again the batter swung with all his might, and again he missed and struck out.

Only this time the pitch also fooled the Stars catcher, kicked off his mitt and rolled to the backstop. The batter took off like a scared rabbit, easily making it safely to first. Rey didn't seem shaken by this temporary setback as up to the plate strode the third batter of the inning. Again Rey got ahead of the count 0-2. He wasted the third pitch for a 1-2 count. On the fourth pitch, he jammed the Angel hitter inside, sawing off his bat. However, the hitter was just quick enough with his bat head to bloop a little pop fly down the right field line that managed to escape the first baseman's glove.

Now, there was still only one out, with runners on first and second base. The unnerved Rey, momentarily lost his composure and walked the fourth Angel's batter on four consecutive pitches—all balls.

Now everyone in the ballpark was fidgeting in their seats, no matter which team they were pulling for. The Stars pitching coach promptly came out to the pitcher's mound to settle his star reliever down. Rey, like his unique first name, had unusual talent for a nineteen-year-old. What he had abundantly in raw ability, was somewhat offset by his lack of experience and maturity in tight scrapes such as these, and sometimes it caught up with him.

You could just hear the veteran pitching coach with both his experienced arms resting on his young phenom's broad shoulders, saying reassuringly, "Del Vaughn, before each pitch take a deep breath, relax and then deliver the pitch with a smooth motion. Don't try to over throw the ball—stay within yourself and go with your best pitch. Got it?"

The phenom answered with a nod of his head and the coach turned and walked back to the home dugout. The catcher and third baseman who had also joined the conference on the mound, both added words of support and returned to their respective positions.

It was up to Rey now. He took a deep breath as he prepared to face the fifth batter of the inning. There was no room for error with the bases loaded and only one out. He determined he would go right at the batter and try to over power him with his money pitch—a 96 mph fastball.

His first pitch was straight down the pipe and made a loud whap as it hit the catcher's mitt. "Strike One," the umpire declared.

His second pitch was belt high and on the inside portion of the plate. There was heard another whap. "Strike Two!" the umpire shouted.

His third pitch was not only the swiftest, it tailed away from the batter as it cut across the black border of home plate. "Strike Three!" the umpire bellowed. The hapless batter was out on three pitches without ever getting the reposed Louisville Slugger off his shoulder.

Rey took another deep breath as he walked off the back of the mound and picked up the resin bag lying on the edge of the grass that circumferenced the mound. He gently fondled it in his pitching hand while gathering his thoughts and calming his emotions. Just one more batter remained to subdue.

The Confrontation

That one remaining batter however, was the most dangerous hitter in the league, Steve Bilko. The scenario which I thought was implausible, was now unfolding right before my face. What an imposing sight, six-foot-one, two-hundred-and-forty-pound veteran, power hitting Bilko, digging in at the plate; and ninety feet in front of home plate, standing resolutely on the pitching rubber, was six-foot-four, two-hundred-and-five-pound power pitching rookie, Rey.

There was a moment when their eyes met and everything stood still. I imagined a similar moment in time might have occurred between Wyatt Earp and Ike Clanton at the legendary OK Corral, just before the guns began blazing and the bullets were flying.

Rey started the confrontation, by coming inside with the heat and Bilko swung mightily and fouled it straight back. "Strike One!" the umpire declared.

The kid had made a good pitch—one down, two to go. Bilko held up his hand to the umpire, meaning he needed a few seconds extra while he dug with his spikes in the batter's box. Now he was settled and cocked his bat behind his right ear, ready for the second pitch.

The Angel base runners sprang into motion just as Rey rocked out of his high kick delivery and rocketed the ball toward the target on the outside portion of the plate. Again there was a swoosh of air as Bilko swung his potent bat. Only, this time there was a crack instead of whap as the ball leapt off of Bilko's bat and arced lazily down the right field line and landed just foul beyond the fence. "Strike Two!" the umpire shouted.

The kid had gotten away with one that time. Bilko's bat was just a fraction slow or that ball would have cleared the fence in fair territory.

The Kid could taste the victory now—he was that close—one more strike. Bilko, the polished veteran wasn't going to be rushed. He took a little stroll over to the on-deck circle, picked up the weighted bat and swung it several times along with his own. He did this almost subconsciously to make his bat seem lighter and hence, just a milli-second quicker.

Then he was ready and stepped back in the box. The kid eyed this ritual with complete detachment. He didn't care what Bilko did, he had known what he was going to throw since he saw that last ball nestle into the fans just foul out in right field. He had perfect confidence in his delivery and in his pitch selection.

Then the moment arrived. Rey rocked back and strided his right foot toward the plate. He released the ball with a fluid energy, this time toward the inner portion of the plate.

Bilko didn't hesitate as he rotated his hips squarely and swiftly brought his strong wrists gripping the bat in an arc through the strike zone—Kaboom! It sounded like a kinetic explosion or a lightning strike nearby. Before anyone realized it, the ball had rocketed over the centerfield fence and into the gathering haze of the late afternoon. Just like that, the score read 6-2 in favor of the LA Angels!

There was a stony silence in the stadium-almost mausoleum like except for the few Angel's fans in attendance who were jubilantly celebrating the amazing turn of events. You could almost imagine yourself in attendance at one of those solemn funerals at Forrest Lawn Memorial Park, when a famous Hollywood star passes away and perfect strangers turn out with bouquets in their hands and tears in their eyes.

I'd seen enough. I got up and headed for the nearest exit. My Stars were about to lose their third consecutive game to the syrupy Los Angeles Angels. It had not been a good homestand. This had not been a profitable day so far for me either. The Hollywood Stars had failed to gain a victory over their rivals, I still had no idea for a story concept, and no birthday present for Mom.

I beat most of the crowd out of the Gilmore Field exits and walked back over to the central section of the Market. I strolled over to the Asian Import House. I thought I might still save the day by finding Mom just the right gift among their exotic import inventory.

Besides, I could always amuse myself by watching the multi-colored Asian turtles playfully diverting themselves in their display aquarium. They were so cute climbing over each other's diminutive bodies that didn't exceed two inches in length. They also sold them in clear plastic circular aquariums that had small islands where the turtles could sun themselves under a plastic palm tree. Now, that was the life for a diminutive green turtle!

This had been a tradition of mine to visit the miniature green turtles and other interesting items found inside the Asian Import House, since Mom first brought me along while she did her shopping. That had been about twenty years earlier. I guess you could say I had grown up at Farmers' Market.

A Girl Named Tanya

I no sooner walked through the bamboo clad entrance, and I was approached by a stunning vision of a young Chinese woman in shimmering blue satin. She was tall, lithesome and the electric blue dress clung perfectly to her comely form as she moved. I could have sworn she came directly from "Central Casting" as a heroine of some "Charlie Chan" mystery. "My name is Chippie, may I help you find a special gift?" For a moment I was too stunned to answer. I finally managed to respond, "Your name is whatie?"

No sooner were the words out of my mouth than I wished I could have recalled them. I couldn't believe I had been so flippant or casual with someone I didn't know. She didn't take offense, she merely smiled cordially and repeated her name. She explained that it was a nickname that several of her American friends gave her soon after she immigrated to the states from China. Then she politely repeated her question, "Is there a special occasion that you're shopping for?"

I answered that I was looking for an unusual gift suitable for my mom's birthday. I could tell that my purpose pleased her by the slightest softening of her delicate features. As she proceeded to ask me general questions about my mom and to suggest a few possible categories of items my mother might enjoy, she abruptly paused and apologized for failing to show me a specific item immediately.

I tried to assure her I appreciated her interest, but before I could, she continued her explanation that in her homeland, gift giving was not nearly so casual a process as it is in America. Especially when the gift was for a dear family member, more thoughtful contemplation was required. The dearer the person was to you, the more precious the gift must be—not in monetary terms, but in consideration of the gift's ideal suitability to express an aspect of uniqueness in the spirit of the individual for whom the gift was intended.

I stood transfixed beside her, having been magically spellbound by her words, her grace, and surely by the magnanimity of her palpable essence. I was staring at her when she became uncomfortable with my silent impingement of her spirit.

She glanced down, and as her eyes fluttered back up to mine, she expressed concern. "Have my thoughts offended you?"

"Not at all," I reassured her. "To the contrary, your openness and sincerity are truly refreshing." Then, I quickly added, "However, you've created a dilemma for me."

She now looked at me questioningly. "I have?"

The Request

"Yes, after listening to your thoughts, I am convinced there is only one person with the requisite wisdom to assist me in this important decision, you!"

"Oh?" she sighed.

"The dilemma is this, there are only five days left till Mom's party this coming Saturday; and as you've so eloquently suggested that only leaves scant time for me to share some informative stories with you about Mom." I paused only a brief moment. "Will you please have dinner with me?"

That wonderfully warm countenance returned to her radiant face.

"I would be delighted, but I don't get off for an hour—is that acceptable?"

"It's perfect." Wow, I exclaimed silently! "I'll meet you back here in an hour." I was beaming like some neophyte schoolboy contemplating his first date, as I left her place of business.

Later, after I had returned Tanya (she had revealed this was her real Christian name) to her waiting roommate by the Market's clock tower to take her home, I reflected on my experiences. While we had eaten dinner at a Chinatown restaurant she recommended, I had studied her as carefully as I could without being obvious. Tanya was captivating to look upon. Her exotic looks hinted that there was some mix of Eurasian genetics, rather than pure Chinese. She definitely was not by temperament the "Dragon Lady" character portrayed in Republic serials—Tanya was simply too genuine, caring and without guile to fit that role.

Tanya, like a beautifully cut gem, was beguiling and complex due to her many positive facets, not in the shadowy, inscrutable manner of a dragon lady in an opium den. She was captivating because of her subtle charms that entranced me, like the art lovers, historians and critics had been for centuries with the remarkable painting of Mona Lisa by Leonardo de Vinci.

There was something of enduring charm and fascination that was caught by Leonardo in his masterful portrait. People from many countries and cultures visit the Louvre Art Museum in Paris, to wait in long lines to view her for a few moments to this day.

Down through the centuries, men have inquired as to what lies hidden behind that most subtle of smiles. In Tanya's case, that intriguing blend of Occidental virtues combined with the allure of the Oriental mystique, was what rendered her irresistible!

Tanya said she would have her suggested gift for my consideration by Friday evening and we arranged to meet again at the Asian Import House just as her shift ended at 7 p.m. She also accepted my invitation to dine with me again, this time at my favorite night spot.

Some Enchanted Evening

Friday evening came quickly and I met Tanya as we had prearranged. On the way to the "Tropic's Isle" restaurant located atop the foothills overlooking Burbank, Glendale, and Hollywood, I noticed a slightly different mood in her demeanor.

Tanya still radiated warmth and the genuine interest in our conversation as was her norm, yet I discerned her spirit was slightly subdued. As we arrived at the "Tropic's Isle," I pulled up to the valet parking where the attendant assisted her out of the car.

It was one of those lovely Southern California nights that the tourism office always likes to promote. It was just a few minutes before eight and a balmy sixty five degrees with a gently caressing breeze that barely moved a strand of her long ebony hair.

I took Tanya's hand and said there was something special I wanted her to see. She instinctively followed as I explained our reservation was for eight, so we had a few minutes and wouldn't be late. I led her to a flowery adorned walkway that ran around the side of the restaurant to a tropical themed sitting environ with burning torches, dwarf palms, several varieties of orchids and birds of paradise.

We sat upon a bamboo and cushioned love seat and gazed upon the romantic vista of a "starry night" straight out of a Van Gogh painting. There were twinkling lights everywhere, from the many residences and streets below to the jeweled heavens above.

I wondered if this celestial treasury of nightly delights would relax Tanya enough that she might share what was on her mind. "I have brought something very special for you to appraise after dinner, as to its suitability for your mother's gift. It may take me ten or fifteen minutes to relate my thoughts to you regarding why I believe this particular item's unique qualities recommend themselves to you in a superior way than any other would. May I suggest we go in for dinner now and perhaps return here afterwards, so that I may present the item to you for your consideration?"

"Of course we can," I responded as I assisted her to her feet and escorted her into the restaurant from the Tropic Isle's lovely tropical garden-patio setting.

As we walked to the maitre d' station, I really noticed for the first time, that she was carrying a large flowered tote bag. The slightly bulging bag obviously contained the subject item.

We were seated at an ideal table near a waterfall that appeared to emerge from a hidden spring inside a natural stone wall. The frothy water cascaded down over moss covered rocks that formed tranquil pools at several levels. The entire rear of the restaurant was enclosed by large pane glass windows which afforded an unobstructed view of the large valley spread out below.

The entire vista and setting were enchanted, but Tanya, as from the time I first beheld her, was the most captivating of all. The dinner was deliciously satisfying and segued into exotic desserts. All the time I pondered, what was the mystical object within her tote bag?

Within minutes I had paid for our dinner and we had returned to our awaiting love seat. "Please, Tanya, I'm about to burst from curiosity. Show me what you have selected" I implored.

She intently looked me in the eyes and firmly responded, "Not until I tell its story of origin and the meaningful circumstances of its coming forth. Would you have me grossly devalue it, by leaving unexpressed its true significance?"

All of a sudden I felt like the ones being referred to in the biblical passage that reads something like, "Cast not your pearls before swine!" I proceeded to say to her, "Take your time, Tanya, and tell me the entire episode from the beginning." I was trying to demonstrate the proper patience and maturity while not seeming stiff or indifferent.

Meanwhile, I was becoming increasingly contemptuous of her formality. Her elegant politeness was one of her undeniable charms. However, on an occasion such as this, I had expected, and indeed hoped for a more relaxed, intimate style of communicating.

The Remarkable Odyssey of LuXuh

As Tanya began relating the remarkable odyssey of her brother, who was twelve years older, I realized this was a proposition that could not be rushed, like fine wine should not be imbibed before its time.

She related how her beloved older brother LuXuh Chin, had excelled in college academics through his freshman and sophomore years at the University of Southern California which he attended on a scholarship to study business and art (he was especially gifted in painting and sculpture). The scholarship had been arranged by the Methodist minister after arriving from America the previous year. Reverend Charles Sinclair served as the pastor of her hometown mission congregation. He had graduated from USC in 1912 with a bachelor's degree in Oriental history and culture followed by a seminary degree. The school had been founded in 1880 in Los Angeles by Methodist church leaders and educators.

After completing the fall semester of his junior year at USC, LuXuh had received an urgent telegram ordering his return to China for enrollment in the newly formed Air Cadet training school. He knew he should feel honored, as only the elite of China's young men were being accepted into this program. It also was an honor to defend one's country against an invading enemy, but he had so hoped to complete his education first.

"Peashooters" vs. "Zeros"

However, the war with Japan wouldn't wait. He consequently returned to China where he excelled as a cadet in pilot training too, graduating at the top of his class in December 1940. Soon He was posted to a fighter squadron and was commissioned a lieutenant in General Chiang Kai-shek's Chinese Nationalist Army Air Corps.

He had even received some joint air combat training with the famed "Flying Tigers" of Colonel Clair Chennault following their arrival in July of 1941. LuXuh had performed exceedingly well in aerial combat with five total victories against the marauding Japanese pilots including: three victories over Mitsubishi Type 96 bombers, one Nakajima Type 96 fighter shot down, and one victory over a Kawasaki Type 93 scout plane.

However, LuXuh had to exercise extreme caution when Japanese fighters were around as they had far superior performance to the obsolete American Boeing P-26A "Peashooters" he and his brave Chinese comrades had been flying in combat since 1940. By the end of 1941, LuXuh was China's third ranking ace with a total of eleven "kills."

He was happy, LuXun expressed in a letter to his mother, that his squadron had been chosen to receive a newer American fighter plane in February. He didn't know which fighter it would ultimately be, but LuXun yearned for the chance to fly the fabled Curtis P-40 "Warhawks" that the AVG (American Volunteer Group) used in running up such an impressive score against the Japanese. Alas, they were in short supply and always went to other nation's air corps with higher priorities.

LuXuh felt well rested as he returned to duty after nearly a month off to rest and recuperate from the constant fatigue of battle.

He had spent his entire leave with his mother and younger sister, Tanya. Like many frontline soldiers, LuXuh had not realized how thoroughly exhausted he was until he got away from the constant stress of nearly daily battle. The stay at home had done him good.

Two more months passed in diligent training with the new fighter aircraft—the Brewster "Buffalo." Frankly, LuXuh was quite disappointed in the capabilities of the Buffalo. In many respects it was only a marginal improvement over the Boeing P-26A they had been flying, and its performance capabilities were certainly less than the formidable Japanese Zero.

At least the "Buffalo" had an enclosed cockpit feature. It was the first time LuXuh had flown a plane without the wind blowing straight into his face as it did in the obsolete "Peashooter." Also, this robust plane could take more punishment and keep flying. The "Buffalo" was slightly faster than the P-26A, but it was a beastly plane to maneuver with sluggish controls. That isn't the formula for success or long life if your adversary is flying "Zeros!" All of this was background information, Tanya informed me, in order that I might better understand the heart of the story.

"We used to hear from LuXuh on a regular basis," Tanya confided. "He was very good about writing to mother every other week from his base in Nanking. His last letter was dated 26 March 1942. In the letter, LuXun stated that after weeks of training and combat maneuvers, they were as prepared as they could be to re-enter combat against the determined Japanese and their top flight military aircraft."

She continued, "Although Mother had tried to conceal her fears from me, I sensed something was not well with LuXuh. We finally received official notification from his commanding officer at Nanking on 8 May 1942 that Luxuh had been shot down and wounded in the shoulder. He had been captured by a Japanese army patrol and imprisoned. Nothing more was known about his condition or location, but the officer promised mother that if and when additional news became available, he would promptly notify her."

The Red Cross Message

"Over a year went by without any further news of LuXuh. Then we were contacted by the American Red Cross on 19 August, 1943 that he was well and was being held at a prison camp near Singapore. The communiqué said LuXuh received slightly better treatment than most because he was an officer and could speak fluent English. The Japanese officers used this to their advantage to assist them in translating during questioning of American POWs, mainly downed flyers like himself." There was a hint of pride and deep affection for her brother in Tanya's expression as she continued her narrative.

She explained that, "This was a flagrant violation of the Geneva Convention on the treatment of prisoners and what they could be required to do by their captors. This did not detour the Japanese who did not recognize the Geneva Convention, nor would they allow any outside organization to bind their hands in getting what they wanted from prisoners. Prisoners who did not follow orders were summarily executed.

"Mother and I were overjoyed to learn after so long that our beloved LuXuh was still alive and receiving at least minimal standards of food, shelter and medical treatment. I will never forget this day as it also marked the occasion of my eleventh birthday. I could not have wished for a better birthday present than this welcome news.

"We dared not let our hopes soar too high regarding his eventual safe return, although we were confident that the Japanese would preserve his life, as long as they found him useful."

Hiroshima POW

"Another fifteen months passed by before we heard again from the American Red Cross on 24 November 1944 regarding LuXuh's status. He had been transferred by freighter from Singapore to another prison camp in Hiroshima, Japan, where there were mostly American air crews with a smattering of others being held.

They also mentioned that this was a safe haven for the prisoners as well as the civilian population as Hiroshima had never been attacked by the large formations of giant American B-29 bombers that had inflicted massive damage to many cities throughout the Japanese home islands."

Tanya then described how the people of her congregation had learned that the war had been going badly for the empire of the rising sun. On all fronts, Japan's forces were suffering defeat after defeat and were being compressed into an ever shrinking circle by American forces. "They had lost the battle for Iwo Jima and as of May 1945," she recalled, "it looked like they would also lose Okinawa." It was to be the last major battle for an island fortress between the Allies and the Empire of Emperor Hirohito.

Her voice then became more animated. "Mother and I prayed daily for a swift end to the war, not only for LuXuh's sake, but for all humanity as well." I had read several books on the war in the Pacific that presented eyewitness accounts that corroborated Tanya's account of how Japanese military forces were every bit as brutal toward noncombatants as was the Third Reich. Like the inhuman Nazi treatment of Jews and others, Japanese officers and soldiers made no distinction between combatants and noncombatants as they slaughtered several million Chinese civilians during the "Rape of Nanking" and elsewhere.

The Reverend Dr. Charles Sinclair

Tanya's eyes always seemed compassionate when she mentioned Dr. Sinclair. "Reverend Sinclair would often pay us a visit to see how Mother and I were doing and to offer a prayer of comfort on our behalf that the war would end swiftly and we would be united with our son and brother. We so enjoyed Reverend Sinclair's visits to our home which always included his comforting words of prayer and encouragement.

"He had such an intuitive understanding of Chinese people in general and of our family in particular. I thought of him as I would my father had I known him before his death. My father had died in the long tragic civil war of China when I was just a year and six months old. He was an adjutant officer to General Chiang Kai-shek, both of whom had a natural affinity for Westerners.

"Through his association with the 'Generalissimo,' Father had become well acquainted with Dr. Sinclair and over time had developed quite a close friendship. Father had even asked Reverend Sinclair to watch over us should anything happen to him. Father also named him executor of the Li family estate which had been passed down to our family from over four hundred years previously. The assets of the estate were quite substantial according to my mother.

"About the same time, Mother and Father accepted the Christian gospel as taught to them by Reverend Sinclair. At the time, Mother did not feel it appropriate to have LuXuh and me baptized. She thought it was too big of a cultural change from the rest of our extended family and friends and that it would be best if we waited until we were old enough to understand the possible ramifications before proceeding. I am happy to say I was eventually baptized by Reverend Sinclair on my tenth birthday."

She then explained why her brother had not also been baptized. "LuXuh never was baptized. He was simply gone most of the time, at the regional school, or in the states and then the war. I believe he still will, it's just the world has been too hectic for a young man like Luxuh to concentrate on anything ethereal—only the demands for excelling or surviving in the moment."

Her narrative then picked up pace. "The night of 5 August 1945, I had just finished writing in my personal journal that I have kept since LuXuh went away to war. I was pondering the future. It seemed to me as though the war would drag on forever.

"I awoke the next morning with a new resolve to be more proactive instead of just waiting helplessly for the days to interminably roll by, one after another. I felt I had to do something to change the status of things, if nothing more than my own attitude.

"I decided to join a group of young people that were meeting this evening at Reverend Sinclair's rectory to discuss a proposed youth outing. Although the war raged on, its frontlines were much more remote from us than they once, not long ago, had been. Dr. Sinclair insisted that we push ahead with our lives in spite of the war, and that included these short retreats where we could develop social skills along with bible study."

"Little Boy"

"When I arrived at the rectory in the afternoon, the place was buzzing. Youth and adults were standing in small clusters discussing the news. Sketchy reports were filtering into China that American military forces had just this morning of 6 August, employed some new bomb of extremely high explosive power against a Japanese city. It was reported that the new weapon effectively destroyed the city."

"No one knew any details. Reports were still coming in to the local news media regarding this stunning development. Everyone was speculating on rather this would bring an end to the intolerable war.

"The Atomic bombing of Hiroshima didn't end the war immediately, but coupled with a second atomic strike on the city of Nagasaki on 9 August, finally, mercifully, induced Japanese Emperor Hirohito and his military leaders to capitulate and accept the unconditional surrender terms on 14 August 1945." Tanya slumped slightly as if it had taken something out of her emotionally to relate this story to me.

Then after breathing deeply, she gathered herself like a runner finding a second wind for the last mile of a marathon and spoke again. "Three months later, LuXuh, at last came home to us. He had been through an ordeal that almost defies description. The day of the attack, LuXuh was fortunately on a prisoner work detail, that had departed Hiroshima before 7 a.m. He, along with thirty other prisoners were working on constructing gun emplacements and other fortifications in the foothills overlooking the city. The Japanese military was preparing for the massive invasion they knew would inevitably come, now that the Empire had lost Okinawa.

"Where LuXuh was laboring was approximately three miles from the point of detonation of 'Little Boy,' the first atomic bomb deployed in war. When the bomb detonated at 8:16 a.m., he was digging a trench and facing away from the blast. Still the flash of fissionable light permeated everything and the shockwave flattened him, even at that distance.

"Once the guards regained their orientation, they hurriedly gathered the prisoners together at rifle point and returned with them to the prison in the northern part of the city." She stopped her riveting narrative momentarily to explain she had once borrowed a book from Dr. Sinclair's library that the good reverend had recommended she read. Dante's *Inferno* had captivated Tanya and she said that her brother's horrific description of the post attack Hiroshima presented a scene straight out of scenes from the book. Continuing with LuXuh's experiences, she said, "The city was in shambles, with roughly seventy percent of the structures flattened or in flames. Out of an estimated population of 320,000, approximately 80,000 people had died instantly or suffered mortal wounds.

"The next day the surviving prisoners were transported by truck to another POW camp in a neighboring community about ten miles distant. LuXuh and others had survived the bomb explosion itself, but what about the radiation exposure? No one knew much about the harmful effects of being exposed for twenty-four hours to the lingering radiation of the first atomic bomb attack." The anguish in her eyes was visible as if she knew the answer and it was unpleasant.

Resolutely, she continued, "He was fortunate to not have been harmed by his captors as some of the American POWs had been killed in retribution for the unprecedented attack. When LuXuh returned home, he was a different man than the perpetually happy young man I knew before the war. He was somber much of the time and introspective. He refused comment on his war experiences.

"Instead, he spent his time almost exclusively, developing his artistic skills that had shown so much prewar potential. He was obsessed with the notion that individuals and nations needed to focus on objects of beauty in nature which encouraged us to love and understand one another rather than mistrust and despise one another. He painted and sculpted. One of his favorite subjects was the owl because he said it possessed a mystical reputation for wisdom among the animal kingdom.

"LuXuh had brought home just one souvenir of his stay in Japan—consisting of several pieces of aqua colored glass that he had found along the sandy banks of the Ota River running through Hiroshima. They were fragments of sand converted to silicon under immense heat and pressure of the atomic blast. He thought they were unusually beautiful and seemed to him the symbols of hope for the future that emerged from the despair and destruction of war.

"Eventually, Luxuh turned to glass blowing, trying as always to capture the simple essence of beauty in his work that he found in what he referred to as his Hiroshima gems!"

Tanya had been relating her brother's story to me for over an hour by this time. Now she took a shallow breath and turned to face me. "That is the background story of the object that I have brought to you as a gift for your dear mother. Although I have not met her, from the stories you've shared with me about her, I feel I know her and how much you love her."

The Gift

As Tanya carefully removed the bundle from her tote bag, she continued, "It cannot be purchased. It is a gift from my brother and me to you and your mother. That is the tradition in China between family members and loved ones.

"I received a long letter from my mother yesterday asking me to come home to be with LuXuh and assist with his care. He has been very ill the past month and the doctors don't know yet what if anything can be done for him. Mother said this was his last piece of art, completed just as he was becoming ill. Now he's too ill to do any more art. It takes all his concentration to fight the illness."

With that, Tanya removed the scarf concealing her brother's last creative expression of hope for tomorrow. It was a beautiful aquamarine colored glass owl—LuXuh's symbol for the beauty and wisdom he found in nature. Tanya said her brother had formed it as a delicate pitcher so that it could always pour out its contents and share that regenerating wisdom with others.

I was dumbstruck at the majestic quality of the gift and profundity of the sentiment behind it. I had never thought of myself as a thoughtless, shallow person, but at the moment I felt like a person that was clueless as to the greater meanings of human relationships and the significance of our time on earth.

I wanted to respond appropriately, but I didn't know what to say. Here I am, a writer, I thought to myself and I'm at a loss for words. The simple truth is, if I had taken the time previously to really think deeply about people and issues, I'd have known what to say in that instance and meant it. I stood convicted by my own inner testimony—I was guilty, as are so many others in America of superficial self-centeredness.

There was only one response I could think of that would express my inner feelings as I gently leaned toward her and softly kissed her. It wasn't a passionate kiss, rather a kiss of compassion born out of the genuine appreciation I felt for this remarkable young lady.

Epilogue

Tanya left Southern California in two days to return to her family that now resided in Taiwan. I took her to Los Angeles International Airport on Sunday where she boarded a flight for the long trip home. Although we spoke confidently about a near future reunion, I had a premonition that this would be the last time I would see Tanya for at least a long time.

After an emotional farewell embrace, I presented Tanya with some parting gifts. In addition to some common gifts that men give to women they esteem, I enclosed a personal letter of hope and appreciation to her brother. Lastly, I composed a letter of gratitude to her mother expressing my deepest respect for her, in having nurtured such a delightfully inspiring individual as Tanya and a wonderfully talented and thoughtful son as LuXuh. I ended the letter by saying I had never personally known anyone of more intrinsic goodness and grace than her daughter.

Tanya and I corresponded weekly for over a year, but as often happens, our letter writing gradually slowed to an occasional letter every four to six months as the demands of life became more complicated and stressful. Her brother LuXuh, finally succumbed to the effects of radiation poisoning after two years of difficult illness; but not before he was baptized. Tanya said he treasured my letter and kept it with him until the day he died.

It is now 1985, thirty years later since that fateful meeting in Farmers' Market. Tanya is now fifty-three years of age and I am fifty-eight. Both Tanya and I were fortunate to eventually meet and fall deeply in love with wonderful people to whom we are now happily married. We are both raising families in a Christian environment that is fulfilling as it is challenging.

She now lives with her spouse, four teenagers, two dogs and a parrot in a spacious rambling ranch home in scenic Hawaii on a bluff over looking the Pacific. Oh yes, Tanya's mother is well and resides with them in a grandma's cottage in their one-acre back yard.

Tanya has continued on with her brother's passion for art and the beauty in life that it can represent. She has created a line of children's books that she both writes and illustrates. She has a growing popularity worldwide. It is quite an accomplishment for a woman that grew up in war-torn China.

We still correspond, sending each other Christmas cards every year with a long newsletter containing all the news about ourselves and our family's latest adventures and surprises of life.

However, nothing surprises me about her to this day. You see, Tanya, was to me, living proof of a loving Creator who dwells in the heavens above. She was herself a gift of Providence, a wonderful example of how beautiful life can be, if we live by the principle of sharing love and wisdom, as does the mythical Wisdom Owl of China (the name Mom affectionately gave to the cherished gift).

PS: I decided against parting with the one of a kind glass owl. How could I have ever contemplated doing so? It simply represented too much of significance to me. I immediately carried it gently upstairs to the family den where my mom's china cabinet had been relocated by my wife. I opened the glass door and restored it to its former place of honor just as it had been for thirty years until Mom's passing.

This Christmas I decided I would tell my four young adult children, the endearing story of the greatest gift Grandma, or indeed our family had ever received—the "Wisdom Owl of China." I would tell them the moving events of the life of the naturalist artist LuXun and of his radiant sister Tanya. I would convey the circumstances of how this precious gift came to be in our possession. I would tell them how this last creative expression of a dying artist, given so selflessly to enrich the life of another, was in similitude of the unconditional love of Christ. In a very special way, it reflected his mission of sacrificial atonement and his gift of eternal life to us and to all of Heavenly Father's children.

Tigers over Rangoon

Colonel Clair Chennault was an officer in the United States Army Air Corps preceding WWII who was out of step with many of his contemporary officers in terms of the prevailing attitudes and strategies of air combat. He was a visionary, and as is so often the case with original thinkers, he was held in low esteem and even contempt by others who lacked vision and were less gifted. His views were original and not harmonious with many of their outmoded ideas on air warfare.

Chennault, like T. E. Lawrence, the British officer who exhibited a keen interest in the future of Arabia during WWI, had a similar passion for the welfare and future of the China and her people in the late 1930s. His interest focused on aiding the air defense of their nation against the invading military forces of Imperial Japan before and during WWII. Chennault's dream was to employ his revolutionary air combat tactics in repulsing the marauding Japanese air armada that for years had reigned down death and terror over much of China. He perceived his mission to be a crusade to defend China from Japan's aggression. He was not afraid to promote his views or to ruffle the feathers of fellow officers or superiors in so doing.

When it became strategically and geo-politically important to the United States War Department officials to lend some kind of clandestine, unofficial military aid to the over-matched Chinese, Chennault's opportunity arrived. Army leaders saw what they perceived to be an ideal and non-threatening way to prove or disprove Chennault's philosophies on modern air combat strategy while also assisting China. He received a dramatic endorsement from President Roosevelt when his idea to form the American Volunteer Group (Flying Tigers) was approved on July 23, 1941.

Chennault was a tough but always fair leader. He believed in cohesive teamwork and stressed this with his pilots. He insisted on and succeeded in getting everyone to do what he wanted under his command. The few who did not were sent home. He built a team that mirrored his own tactical thinking and complete dedication to the cause for which they were in China. After a career of planning his tactics, the opportunity finally arrived for him and his Tigers to show what they could do. He had at his disposal 90 planes and 86 pilots which faced an imposing 1500 Japanese planes on the mainland of Indo-China.

What resulted was the most remarkable and one-sided victory in the history of air combat. During the Christmas week following Pearl Harbor, occurred the dramatic air battle of Rangoon where the Flying Tigers succeeded in destroying 62 Japanese planes while the A.V.G. (American Volunteer Group) lost only two.

Throughout their history, the A.V.G. regularly faced upwards of 20 to 1 odds. If that was not enough, Chennault and his men had to deal with far less than optimistic conditions in terms of crude facilities and short supplies of ammunition, aviation fuel, spare parts, replacement planes and pilots. In spite of all of this, Chennault and the Flying Tigers achieved the difficult, if not impossible objectives they were assigned. It was a record of accomplishment on the ground and in the air that most likely will never be equaled, let alone surpassed.

Chennault and the AVG he built were stirring and quintessential examples of the unique American can-do spirit that permeated the generation that confronted and defeated both the ravages of the great depression and the global Axis threat to liberty. Six decades later, we need to recall that spirit more than any previous time since Chennault and his "Flying Tiger" boys passed into history.

A Sailor's Odyssey

Oh my brave and noble son,
off you go so resolute,
Sailing away
from San Diego's comely breezes
and gently swaying palms,
from loving wife and newborn son,
leaving them in a spreading wake,
sailing away, from tranquil shores of San Diego.

Shipping out to far away ports o' call
and to Pacific fleet rendezvous,
your thoughts drift back
through salty tears of parting
to when you first met her,
a guiless farm girl in floral dress
and you the dashing trumpet player
with broad lapels and painted tie.

It was love
at first sight and so…
soon thereafter you were married,
and the two of you set your course,
you playing your golden horn
and she, the loving bride watching you
across the dance floor was contented.

Those were
easygoing pleasant days of
many cherished memories in the heartland
of Kansas and Iowa,
of the tall beautiful farm girl with flowing black hair
and the dashing trumpet player.

Until over the radio one peaceful Sunday noon,
came the dreadful news of Pearl being bombed,
and you sensed
your life would forever be changing.

And now sailing away over turbulent seas
and lonely weeks of pensive restlessness,
at last you've come to anchor offshore—
the enemy held island of your impending destiny.

How deceiving
the vista of sandy beaches
and gentle breezes,
of swaying palms in the moonlight—
until disrupted by naval fire
and eruptions of cascading bombs,
the frightful cacophony of combat opened your eyes
to bloody, surreal conflict.

Storming Okinawa's foreboding shore,
brave marines and soldiers land unopposed
and through their first invasion day
spend many a wary hour securing the landing from counter attack.
The agenda of the second day sees our combat teams
tenuously moving inland to confront the forces of Imperial Japan.
Yet, the stealthy enemy remains concealed,
waiting for just the right moment, waiting…
and on the third invasion day purgatory's fire breaks loose,
at last the hidden enemy joins the battle
with many exploding cannon and mortar shells raining down.
Our men held their ground in the face of this withering fire
that seemed to come from nearly every direction.
But, by the end of the day many a brave marine
and soldier was found crumpled on the ground,
dead or dying where he lay.

Out to you
waiting on your mercy ship,
comes the urgent call for aid.
In an instant you swing into action,
giving medical care to the wounded
and heart felt consolation.

All broken, torn and wounded,
you can sew their wounds together again
and mend the broken parts;
but can you apply enough soothing balm
to ever restore their peace of mind,
following the unmitigated horrors of Pacific war.

A "Divine Wind"
these sons of Nippon fanatically called it,
as American sailors and airmen too,
came under attack from the foreboding sky.
Wave after wave of Kamikazes came hurtling in,
laden with fuel and bombs
they dove their Zero planes
into hapless, exploding ships
and sent them down—split in two...
down to silent death,
down in the depths of Davy Jones' locker.

And what about you
as day after day
you faithfully manned your action station—
a pharmacy mate,
powerless to stop the horrific carnage.
All you could do is dress their wounds,
or prepare them for surgery
as they cried from pain,
"Oh please, God, give me Mercy!"

And so you rendered
all the care you possibly could,
to relieve their torment and suffering...
you poured your heart and soul into them.
Caring for them within the bowels of your mercy ship,
you hoped to make them whole again.

Day after day
your maddening routine never changed.
How long could this brutal Okinawa campaign
continue on you wondered?
Outside the sounds of destruction echoed on and on—
days into weeks—weeks into months.
The battle tested sons of Nippon rather than surrender,
chose to triumph or die and bonsai charged
like mystic samurai from the rising sun!
Thus, one of the fiercest battles in WWII raged relentlessly on.

With each passing day you doubted
your ability to carry on,
tending these poor, bloody bastards—
these woeful, anguished men,
can you imagine;
these tragic, yet heroic figures
lying broken in hundreds of bunks and cots
awaited your tender care and compassionate words.
These wounded warriors thought of you,
who never fired a shot or tossed a grenade in anger,
as their abiding, compassionate hero.
Can you imagine?

At last after 83 days of harrowing conflict
the battle for Okinawa ended.
More than a quarter million souls had perished,
nearly all of Hirohito's imperial soldiers and tragically,

over 150,000 Okinawa civilians
held captive by the Japanese;
and oh yes,
Americans suffered mightily too—
fifty thousand casualties—many of whom you attended.

Your hospital ship at last weighed anchor
and sailed away from the harried island combat scene
with you still faithfully tending the wounded.
Until at last your mercy ship
emblazoned with the large red cross,
passed under the "Golden Gate"
and delivered its precious human cargo.
Into the waiting arms of anxious loved ones
they were tenderly received.

You were proud of them
as they waved farewell to you,
and with some temerity left your mercy ship—
some hobbling on crutches,
some being carried in litters.
A tear came to your eye
as you reflected on their painful travails—
these heroic men of war
who'd received medals galore—
Purple Hearts and Medals of Honor
for distinguished valor.

Yes,
you were happy for them,
'cause they were home from the war
these valorous men,
who vouchsafed our liberty
with their blood...

They had been delivered home to waiting, appreciative arms,
of wives, mothers and fathers,
so consoling.

And what of you,
who had campaign ribbons on your chest,
though no Purple Heart or Medals of Honor—
to signify how much you'd given
of yourself to save the lives and sanity of others.

Your lovely wife and one-year-old son
were also there waiting with open arms,
just like the spouses of the maimed,
to welcome you home in triumph…
home from the eternal sea
and endless struggles against the forces of tyranny.

She threw her arms around you,
and whispered…
"Oh, honey,
you're home at last—
it's peace…the war is over!"

Yes,
the war was over,
Japan had at last surrendered unconditionally.
Yet, there waged a conflict within you—
a bloodless one that was unsettling…
dreams of flaming ships sinking beneath the waves,
dreams of crying, terribly anguished men,
heroic men torn apart in battle…
unto them you gave your all
to save their lives,
and restore their limbs.

You tried to resume
your "Big Band" career—
playing your golden horn,
but alas,
your trumpeter's strong lip had long since fled
and so had your drive to reclaim it.

Every time
you tried to sleep or close your eyes,
those same apparitions reappeared,
those blank faces of the dead devoid of animated expression...
the hundreds you treated but couldn't repair,
the ones you reluctantly buried at sea.

The instruments of peace had been witnessed
and signed on the decks of the Mighty Mo in Tokyo Harbor.
The war in the Pacific was officially over,
but, not for the likes of you.
They were always there—
in your mind you saw them slumbering
six fathoms down,
at peaceful rest in Davy Jones' Locker.
They were the fortunate ones,
the only ones truly at peace...
asleep and oblivious to terrors six fathoms down
in Davy Jones' locker.

No matter how hard you tried
everything went awry...
and so you drank a few beers
in any convenient neighborhood bar,
and commiserated with any willing ear,
trying to forget the horrors of war
and the men you couldn't forget,
the men with expressionless faces.

After several years of fruitless jobs,
of moving here and there,
the marriage ended on the rocks
and you departed wife and six year old son…
with the hope of finding peace
in other faces and distant places.

I only knew you briefly from one fleeting reunion
before you died at sixty-five.
I was told you died of a broken heart
and of recriminating regret for the failed life you felt you'd led;
but let me tell you, Dad,
in my heart you'll always be my everlasting hero.

I honor your memory
regardless of non awarded Purple Hearts
or Medals of Honor for distinguished bravery.
I know what you sacrificed to preserve our nation's
endangered liberty
and many a man's precious health and precarious sanity;
just as many others of your generation sailed away
to fight and die in foreign lands and on hostile islands.

You gave your heart, your soul,
your very essence to secure for us
the precious blessings we celebrate each July fourth
and hopefully, many more into the future,
as long as this God fearing nation of resolute men,
continues to produce faithful, humanitarian souls
heroic like yours—Semper Fidelis!

Way up in the Sky

Way up in the sky
5,000 feet up
American airmen flying so high,
risking their lives—doing or die,
to bring to an end this horrific, malignant war.
Oh, tell me if you can, where does brutal nationality end
and blessed humanity begin?

Now,
intellectuals said
this new weapon was superfluous,
the Japanese were beaten already,
just exercise patience;
wait and see they'll capitulate yet,
just wait a couple months more—
you'll see.

That's what they said in '45
and still to this day maintain…
we dropped the bombs on them needlessly,
because of slant eyes, sloping brows
and yellow skin claim they,
believe it or not—that's what they say!

Way up in the sky
passing over Iwo Jima
American airmen of the 509th Composite Group flying so high,
once and for all to end the terrible human carnage of WWII,
that had begun four years before
at Pearl, Wake, the Aleutians, Bataan, and Corregidor.

Two explosive experts aboard the B-29 "Enola Gay"
had carefully armed "Little Boy"
as onward to the "Land
of the Rising Sun" they resolutely flew.

"There was no need for operational fission"
was the intellectual's battle cry—
just allow the Los Alamos
scientists led by Szilard to arrange a
peaceful demonstration.
The Japanese militarists would surely see
the futility of further waging war
and eagerly take pen in hand
to sign the documents of peace said they.
Thus, would be ended years of Asian hostilities—
of Japan's ruthless aggression and brutal expansion.

The Japanese generals
led by minister Tojo and others,
saw no wrong in what they were doing.
Their incursions into China, Burma and Malaysia
were merely beneficial endeavors
to establish an "Asia Co-Prosperity Sphere."
"Asia for Asians—No more whites!"
was their propagandistic rational.

When those countries objected to Japan's
self-serving actions to steal their resources
of tin, rubber and petroleum,
and began to defend themselves,
Tojo and his militant generals were hurt,
their sincere intentions had been misunderstood.

So, they sent "The Tiger of Malaysia"
General Yamashita as their emissary
to make matters perfectly clear—
they only wanted what was best for them!

And when General Chiang Kai-Shek
led his Nationalist forces in resisting them,
once again the Japanese turned brutal...
pillaging villages of north and eastern China,
and capturing Shanghai.
Still Chiang and his Nationalist army wouldn't
give in and turn China over to these
criminal men...these so-called
purveyors of Asian prosperity.

This outraged the militarists,
so they ordered a new high in barbarism
to teach the Chinese a lesson...
and when Japanese forces led by the sadist General Nakajima,
reached the capital city of Nanking—
they butchered the men, killed the children,
and raped the women!

Over 200,000 helpless civilians perished in this
merciless slaughter...while more than 20,000
Chinese women were tortured and raped—
night after day the atrocities mounted.
That's what they did for them in 1937
and more of the same in other places in '38, '39, '40, '41
and through to the end of the war.
Yes, so commanded the Japanese Generals
and on marched and fought their brave samurai fighting men,
in order that they might establish their
benevolent co-prosperity sphere!

And because we Allies:
the British, the Canadians, the Dutch, the Americans and others,
objected to their rampaging brutality,
and setting asunder any pretense to observing international law—
they laid plans to attack us too.
So they did in December of 1941 without warning.
On the morning of the infamous 7th,
out of the rising sun they dove
and bombed and strafed the hell out of us…
at Pearl, Wake, and Guam,
at the Philippines and Aleutians.
They bombed our planes to smithereens,
and torpedoed our ships at anchor—
killing thousands of men still asleep in their bunks,
as in the case of the venerable USS *Arizona*.
She was nearly blown clean out of the water
and sank with a crew of dead sailors still asleep—
only now eternally so,
on a lovely peaceful Sunday morning
when we were not at war!

Way up in the sky
over 30,000 feet high
American airmen flying in the "Enola Gay"
neared their target,
"Ten minutes to AP," announced the navigator.
Onward toward destiny the Enola Gay droned
at 200 mph and still climbing…
and snug in her bomb bay "Little Boy" waited
to release his pent-up fury…
thanks to the genius of men as Einstein,
Oppenheimer, Fermi, Bohr and Teller.

It was a black day in early '42
when our besieged soldiers on Bataan
weak from wounds, dysentery and lack of food,
finally surrendered to Japanese forces and hoped for
humanitarian treatment as prisoners of war.
However, the Japanese had other ideas...
and marched these weary laden, sickly men
without rest or water twenty miles a day,
and if any fell out along the way—
as hundreds and hundreds inevitably did,
these brave Nippon sons of Samurai,
according to their noble Bushido code,
bayoneted them where they lay—crying for mercy.
Without thought these mindless hounds of Hell,
spat on the crumpled corpses and walked away...
smug in the knowledge of what their generals had taught them—
that they were descendent from gods while all white
westerners were effete
and weakly of will and soul...
and mete for harshest bondage or death
and little more.

Way up in the sky
above 31,000 feet
Col. Tibbets and his crew of the "Enola Gay" were flying high.
The navigator called Tibbets at 8:12 a.m., and announced "IP!"

Van Kirk had navigated the B-29
to the initial aiming point above Hiroshima.
Now, it wouldn't be long
and at 8:14 a.m. Col. Tibbets commanded
over the intercom, "On Glasses!"
"Stand by for the tone break and the turn."

Bombardier Ferebee made his final deft adjustments,
fifteen seconds till release...
at 8:15 and seventeen seconds
the "Enola Gay's" bomb bay doors sprang open...
"Bomb away," yelled Ferebee
and at once it plummeted down.
"Little Boy" dropped with a sonic roar,
twenty seconds till detonation...
while Tibbets put "Enola Gay" into a severe
right-handed power dive that took the plane five miles away...
at the exact time of 8:16...

Emperor Hirohito
generally preferred peace to war.
Yet was he so aloof from his people
and removed from the day to day affairs of his country...
that human frailty led to negligence of false godliness
allowing the high command of
army generals and minister Tojo a free hand
in conducting a most brutal war of expansion.

In the operational theaters of war,
abroad from the awareness of the folks at home,
their unwavering Samurai fighting men carried out the
militarist's will,
including atrocities galore—too many to enumerate—
where millions upon millions met a hellishly cruel fate.
And all of this the Japanese generals said
was in honor of the Showa Emperor (Hirohito),
a god who walked among men
or so they said.

At 8:16 a.m.
"Little Boy" detonated…
in a flash of atomic heat.
In a second or less,
80,000 soldiers and civilians
were vaporized, incinerated or mortally wounded.
Pitiful survivors with painfully burned and swollen faces and
charred extremities wandered with vacant expressions through
the decimated streets
of the hypocenter that had been a bustling city.
Two thirds of Hiroshima lay flattened…
rubble, smoke and fire everywhere,
and the "Enola Gay" upon circling the city
observed the carnage,
then with her sobered and relieved crew—
banked away and returned safely to her island base on Tinian.

In Tokyo,
when news of the destruction of Hiroshima
by a new type of American weapon
reached the ruling council of ministers and generals,
still they refused to accept the
Allied terms of non-negotiable surrender.
As they had on previous occasions,
they rebuffed all overtures for peace
in preference for fighting on and thus honoring their Bushido code.
Heartlessly ignoring all warnings of coming destruction…
they were ultimately willing to sacrifice
ten million Japanese souls or more.
The generals said among themselves…
we must drag this war out two years or more,
even if it means every Japanese citizen
must give his life for the Emperor…
all to avoid the inevitable—unconditional surrender!

Three days later,
after the second bomb—named "Fat Man"
obliterated half of Nagasaki—
with shocking stories of blackened corpses lying everywhere,
and walking dead with torn shreds of skin hanging down…
still they debated among themselves, yet refusing to capitulate.
Three whole days and nights more they deliberated.
Finally, the Emperor,
not wishing to see his people suffer more,
summoned his belated courage, stepped in and declared
"We must bear the unbearable…"
With that, the ruling council reluctantly conceded—
there would be an end to the Pacific war.

However,
not all the Japanese militarists were disposed to let it go at that,
and high-ranking army officials conspired to
dethrone their deistic Emperor,
a god to them no more.
Hence, sought these evil conspiring men,
to impose their secret marshaled will upon the
land of the rising sun;
and their unsuspecting, wounded and wearied people…
who all these years believed the propagandistic news—
that was carefully prepared and given them…
that Japan was winning the war.

By the pluck of fortuitous fate,
the plot to assassinate the Emperor
was revealed and this last gasp
of mindless terror prudently defeated.

On August 15, the divine monarch
of the Chrysanthemum throne addressed his people,
using such formal words and not mentioning surrender—
most Japanese failed to comprehend
the full meaning of his message…
but one thing they correctly surmised,
they were no longer winning the war.

In most hamlets, towns, and cities throughout Japan
where American servicemen visited,
they were greeted with friendship,
but this was not uniformly the case in Hiroshima or Nagasaki
as one can easily understand.
Years later one survivor of Nagasaki related,
"War is a terrible ordeal
without many rules, we understand,
but what happened to us was beyond
all the broadest of parameters."

What she believed true in her heart
can be understood, yet she
was without knowledge of all the picture.
The great human tragedy of Hiroshima and Nagasaki
cannot be adequately and judiciously understood
apart from the context of the entire Asian-Pacific War
that was initiated by the lustful,
expansion seeking Japanese militarists.
They coveted their neighbor's natural resources which they
lacked at home.
Everywhere the Japanese soldiers marched,
countless war crimes of the most brutal kind were committed.

It was always the same in every nation
or island the Nipponese invaded,
death and destruction followed quickly
to any who stood in their imperial way.
Even prisoners of war, women and children too,
none escaped their criminal brutality throughout Asia or the Pacific.
The Samurai soldiers of Japan,
believed their enemies were inferior beings
and deserved to be treated with disdain.
After all, the Nipponese soldier represented a sacred land
and an Emperor who was god and clearly felt no remorse
whenever it suited him to wield a samurai sword
and remove a helpless enemy's head.

Years later all the facts of Japan's
nefarious war crimes behavior,
was conveniently overlooked by
many sophists, educators, intellectuals,
journalists and pseudo moralists—
and swept under the carpet of revisionist history.

United they claimed that we Americans were
anti humanists, we hated people of color
didn't you know.
That's why we employed the remorseless bombs on
Japanese civilians to end the war…
we were racists who lusted for revenge
didn't you know.
Oh, how deceptive to so many of subsequent generations…
when so called truth is a lie.

But one thing is true,
millions of citizens of America and Japan are alive today,
because the bombs ended the war abruptly—

and those one million American casualties predicted for our forces
preparing to invade the land of rising sun...
and perhaps twice that many predicted for those
defending the Home Islands of Imperial Japan never died,
because Operation Olympic-Coronet never took place...
thanks to the men of Los Alamos who split atoms.

And also to the American
509th Composite Group airmen of the USAAF
flying way up in the sky,
risking their lives on a wing and a prayer,
to deliver a powerful new weapon,
bringing an abrupt end to this malignant war,
thus saving countless lives on both of these opposing sides.

Sleeping, isolationist America
who hated the very thought of war,
nonetheless was awakened rudely
from her dream of abiding far away in peace,
by devoted Japanese Samurai airmen
dropping bombs from a clear blue Sunday morning sky —
dealing death to unsuspecting civilians and servicemen too.
Nearly four years later, Japan suffered a horrific collateral fate
by a handful of courageous American airmen
who had what it took...to drop the Atomic bombs and end the war!

Oh, tell me if you can, when does brutal nationality end,
and blessed humanity begin?
It begins when men's hearts are cleansed of all traces of deceit
or coveting other's lands and possessions and is replaced by
charity for all,
regardless of nationality, religion or color;
as when the Lord Jesus ushers in his prophesied millennium
of peace.

Until then, when all men manifest the grace of God in their hearts,
some men must stand ready to fly way up in the sky
as the angels do,
in defense of God's precious gift to all men of hallowed liberty!

Animals Are People Too

Monkeys and Bananas

Have you ever thought
how alike to monkeys
we are?
Oh, yes,
much we have in common
with these mirthful primates
gifted with prehensile tails
that function in many utilitarian ways.

Not unlike our many ingenious human instrumentalities,
a monkey's tail is indispensable in his or her arboreal world—
an environment where sometimes
one's life is turned upside down
on the capricious moment
of a monkey's often spontaneous needs.

Many a monkey's tail
has saved their furry hide from a precipitous fall
off a precarious lofty perch when strong winds blow,
and shake their heavens, branches and leaves mightily to and fro.
On other heart pounding occasions,
that flexible and furry tool has aided them in rapid flight
from the ravenous appetite and gaping jaws
of some stealthy predator in the dead of night.
'Cause you know, no shortage there be of lowly,
earth hugging creatures hoping to find an unsuspecting monkey
sleeping with contented countenance and plump stomach
full of just consumed banana mash.

My, oh my,
how monkeys love bananas by the bunch—
like bread made from grain,
the staff of life to human kind,
they eat them ripe or green,
they eat them anytime,
day or night—when it's hot or cold,
in the midst of baking summer days or long, wintry nights.
And never do they tire
of peeling and eating them to their endless delight.

A monkey's life is full of joyful mirth,
of playful teasing, of obsessive observing,
of masterful mimicking and diverse role-playing.
That's the inherent primate skill
that says "Hey, look at me, I can be just like you!"
What a monkey really thinks is rarely understood
by us average folks,
unless you possess the remarkable communication skills
of an empathic Dr. Goodall, Dr. Dolittle or Dr. Seuss.

However,
what that says about us is also worth noting,
as we seek acceptance in a human zoo
and in so doing sometimes sacrifice
our priceless and providentially appointed originality.
And why do we thus?
Why, it's quite clear, though nonetheless superficial,
the lengths we humans will go to in order to avoid painful ridicule,
or ostracism from those "Gate Keepers" in the know.
It appears to me, that in so doing we forfeit
individual creative expression
and relegate ourselves to meaningless lives.
Yes we do.

We happily, unwittingly, relegate ourselves to become as
captive monkeys;
who no more than mimic the shallow gestures
of others passing by,
while endlessly eating bananas in a human zoo.

Pelicans in the Zoo

Pelicans float aloft
riding a careless breeze,
always glancing down
to the ocean's windswept surface,
in order to spy
an unsuspecting fish or two or three.

And when they do...
down they plummet from the heights of azure sky,
to scoop aloft some finful delicacy by way of their open beak,
beneath which seems suspended a flexible spacious satchel.

You'll rarely see Pelicans in the zoo
'cause they're not feathered royalty,
not at least in the noble company
of handsome Eagles or soaring Hawks,
or Peacocks so prestigiously plumed.
Nor can they compare in ostentatious beauty
to the pinkish hues of long legged Flamingos,
like those that grace the entrance
to the world famous San Diego Zoo.

Yes,
the unsightly Pelican
seems to me rather aptly named—
for it sounds like a seafaring fowl
that waddles around the docks and beaches,
seeking an edible human handout
of discarded fish or bread if it's free.
It's a scavenger's delight,
perfectly placating a Pelican's conservational nature—

having conserved the energy
of winging far out from land
in search of some morsel
from the endless sea.

No,
the Pelican wouldn't be mistaken
as a rakish bird of prey like a fighting Falcon.
And the plucky Pelican surely lacks the color
and vibrant hues of the brightly festooned Cardinal.
Nor does it possess the fastidiousness
demonstrated in a carefully prepared nest
by the industrious Finch.

But,
if you were to prematurely dismiss
the Pelican as a total repugnant mess,
you'd do so erroneously.
Surely it has a fleshy sack hanging from
its lower beak like a giant jowl,
yet it works so efficiently…
like a grocery bag carrying its haul
of fish for the day.

And with just a flap or two of its wide spreading wings—
propels itself into lofty volumes of boundless air almost effortlessly.
Once it achieves its airborne status,
the Pelican assumes a graceful identity
and is free to dip and climb majestically.
Clearly, it's the equal in resplendent flight
and nature's appointed efficiencies,
as any other feathered fowl
over patchwork land or restless sea.

And one last thought you might contemplate.
There is something that this unpretentious bird
has the other more glamorous ones do not...
the ability to make us feel warm inside.
In all her creative wisdom it is clearly evident
that even Mother Nature appreciates the healing balm that
the mirthful sight of a lovable Pelican can do for the stressed
out among us.

Knowingly,
she has endowed a somewhat funny looking creature
as the Pelican with a subtle purpose in being.
In addition to her excellence in evolutionary design
and surely not the least of Pelican traits,
is a hint of warmth and mirthful personality —
bespeaking a hint of divine humor unique in it,
from all of Mother Nature's other creativity.

Andy, the Cat in the Fort of Old Monterey

Here, in the Fort of Old Monterey
I serve the soldier men
as the assistant to the sergeant of the grounds
who reports to Lieutenant Bailey
every evening at 6 p.m. and then is off again till 8 a.m. the
following day.

Every week night,
I resolutely patrol my assigned duty areas till the first light of dawn.
Dressed in my furry suit of smoky-gray with white trim,
I nobly march the grounds keeping a watchful eye,
making sure all is secure,
here in the Fort of Old Monterey.

My name is Andy,
err, sentry Andy to you as you see,
I guard the approaches to the more substantial
enlisted men's edifices
upon the grounds in the Fort of Old Monterey.
I take pride in my carefully performed rodent patrol
as nary a wily mouse or lumbering rat gets by me,
to take up residence under foot of the army men
who frequent the popular base PX, cinema palace and gymnasium.
I am especially proud of my time-honored record of impen-
etrable guarding of the soldier's mess hall and vital food stuffs,
as well as the officer's headquarters building,
here in the Fort of Old Monterey.

A younger, less experienced cat
is assigned to guard the motor pool, armory, supply depot, etc.
I have the choicest of installation assignments,

171

you clearly see, due to my superior intellect and valued seniority.
My duty isn't very tough and on most clear nights
when the moon is shining, it is rather remarkably routine.
However, on those frequent seasonal occasions
of inclement weather
when the foreboding clouds roll in from above the wind
tossed waves of the tempest bay,
(when I must be most alert)
that's when things become interesting within the imposing walls
surrounding the Fort of Old Monterey.

You see,
without the illuminating rays of the moon
to clearly delineate the various building configurations and
passageways,
I must be especially and keenly attuned in night vision
to any irregular movement or barely perceptible, audible sound.
For surely, these indicate my smaller four-footed friends
have stealthily come a calling.

Yes, when it is obscure and rainy,
these rodent varmints invariably choose to attack.
These are the times that try sentry cat's souls,
who must keep the artful dodgers at bay,
to prohibit them from stealthily entering in,
their mischief to parlay.
To consume a robber's repast or other nefarious gnawing
and burrowing to many a soldier's dismay is their objective,
here in the Fort of Old Monterey.

When I was younger
I took glee in chasing these pesky rodents
from pillar to post and back again hour after hour,
till they tired of my hot pursuit
and reluctantly faded away before the dawning rays.

Now that I am ten, I've become incrementally wiser.
I now smugly employ my superior cunning and brain to lie in
wait for them
at strategic spots along the myriad halls and exterior walkways;
and at just the right moment, out I'll fly
at them unsuspecting rascals.
With a throaty growl and my tail all fluffed,
I present quite an ominous specter!
Off they scurry with tails straight out and whiskers bent back,
destined it seems to break the sound barrier,
here in the Fort of Old Monterey.

Sergeant Robert Haney always has a fresh bowl of cream
and another of nutritious cat food waiting for me
when I come into his office after completing my nightly
guardian vigil.
He affectionately gathers me up to his lap and pets me warmly.
He never fails to take me home to his family over the weekends,
where I play with his two teenage children Becky and Bobby.
I especially enjoy this time with the family,
as I have no duties to perform and bask in every luxurious moment.
While regaling in their bounteous affection,
Jean, his perky wife, always sees I have a can of tasty tuna—
oh, what a delightful life this family affords me!

In just a matter of a few months,
Sergeant Haney will be retiring from the army
after twenty years of faithful service.
He has assured me that I will be accompanying him home
to take up my permanent retirement with him
at the family residence.
I can readily envision myself now,
a fat cat reclining on a soft sofa,
my only duty to purr contentedly as one or the other family member
pats my head or strokes my fulsome tummy—
hour upon endless hour.

I've enjoyed my decade of service here,
within these historic military complex walls.
I often marched alongside neatly formed flanks of uniformed men
or checked out the insides of tanks for any rodent hostels.
Competently, I stood nightly constant vigil,
protecting the various structures from unwanted micely intrusions,
here in the Fort of Old Monterey.

It's been quite a life I've led to this point,
there was the time years ago when the general's speeding staff car
ran over the tip of my tail and I let out a high-pitched howl;
and the time the prop wash from a landing helicopter kicked up dirt
and mud from a nearby pond where I unsuspectingly lay
gathering a few rays in the haze of a summer day,
only to awake covered in varying shades of brackish goop.
One look at my matted, discolored fur
and all the base personnel let out a hilarious roar—
wondering aloud what mission objective required
that I be in army camouflage attired?

Yes, I've quite a few fond memories
from a decade of living in this historic place,
of service to uniformed men
and the officers who commanded them.
However now, I look forward
to an even better more joyful, contented civilian life,
smack in the center of the adoring circle of my adopted
Haney family—
Robert, Jean, Becky and Bobby jr.

Yet, as sure as my name is Andy,
I'll never forget the memories I've acquired while standing post;
and playing, sleeping and living among the many friendly
soldiers I knew best,
here in the Fort of Old Monterey.

Americana: Heroes, Themes and Places

The American Cause of Liberty

What if…
way back then
in 1775,
American patriots
had been unwilling
to pay the price of liberty?

Have you ever considered
where we and the rest
of the world would be today…
if there had not been resolute men
as Patrick Henry whose words
"give me liberty, or give me death!"
inspired his countrymen.

Stirring sentiments as these
fostered their steadfastness,
as when a British force of
seven hundred highly trained soldiers
marched threateningly on the colonists
at Lexington and Concord.

Paul Revere had ridden
from Boston
to spread the alarm,
the British were coming…
and to alert Samuel Adams
and John Hancock,
two prominent leaders of colonial men.

As the British forces approached,
they were hastily met
by sixty valiant Minutemen
and their leader,
Captain John Parker—
who warned his men not to fire first,
and then resolutely added—
"But, if they mean to have war,
let it begin here."

Then a shot rang out,
"The shot heard round the world."
The British fired and fired some more
and a few minutes later,
eight American Minutemen lay dead
on Lexington's grass
and ten others grievously wounded.

Who could have known,
that this little skirmish
would mark the beginning of
the American Revolutionary War.
This modern-day conflict of David versus Goliath
became the quintessential struggle to see if at last,
common man would enjoy the fruits of liberty.

And not long thereafter
ensued the Battle of Concord,
however, this time the Minutemen
were better prepared,
and they caused the British to retreat
from off the bridge at Concord,
back to Lexington,
peppering them with hot lead
as they fled.

More and more Americans
rallied to the Minutemen's call—
nearly four thousand in all,
pursuing the British
all the way back to Boston.
Firing from behind trees and walls of stone,
the upstart Americans shot the Redcoats
full of holes.

Other battles followed
and by summer of 1776,
it was time for true patriots
to be counted and to formally
sever the century old ties to
King George and Great Britain.

In Philadelphia they met,
representing thirteen colonies,
attorneys, merchants and farmers.
Being of like mind and determined,
they assigned Thomas Jefferson the task
of placing into words
what they felt in their hearts—
this passionate yearning to be free of tyranny
that coursed through their veins
as surely as their living blood.

And this assemblage
of earnest, noble men
approved the inspired writings
of Jefferson—with only slight changes,
contained within this profound
Declaration of Independence.
Beginning with these immortal words:
"We hold these truths to be self-evident,

that all men are created equal,
that they are endowed by their Creator
with certain unalienable Rights,
that among these are Life,
Liberty, and the pursuit of Happiness..."

And ending with these:
"And for support of this Declaration,
with a firm reliance on the protection
of Divine Providence,
We mutually pledge to each other
our Lives, our Fortunes,
and our sacred Honor."
A priceless concept of man's individual dignity
and providentially endowed liberty had been born.

Now what began at Lexington
and Concord, spread like flame
throughout the colonies
fueled by the lofty words
of the Declaration
and those of other patriots...
like Thomas Payne's "Common Sense,"
and the aura of virtue
and leadership of General
George Washington.

As the Americans fought,
valor was displayed in many places,
such as Bunker Hill...
where it was said, "Do not fire
until you see the whites of their eyes."
And too there was the resilience of the
Continental Army as they suffered
through the deprivation

of the harshest of winters of '77-'78.
Oh, how they suffered at Valley Forge,
lacking sufficient food, blankets and clothing.
The name of the encampment rang true—
for it forged Washington's men
into a fighting unit with esprit de corp.

Victories came at sundry times,
few and far between.
Yet, there was the victory in '77
over General Burgoyne and his British troops
at the Battle of Saratoga.

Then the fates became a fickle friend—
while the outcome of the war hung in balance;
and was nearly lost at West Point on the Hudson
by the treachery of Benedict Arnold.

Then was received the unsettling news
of a glaring defeat at Camden, South Carolina—
of Americans under command of Gates
dispatched by "Red Coats" of British General Cornwallis.

Not all was lost though,
and in October of '80
the war took a turn for the better,
when the "boys in buckskins"
down south,
defeated the British
at King's Mountain.

That desperate American victory
was followed by another,
as American General Morgan defeated
the British under Tarleton
at Cowpens, South Carolina.

The Americans knew that the course
they had embarked on was true,
and the almighty hand of Providence
was sustaining them...
so on they trudged—
persevering on faith in the God
of Abraham, Isaac and Jacob,
for the promised blood and hope of Joseph
of ancient Egypt was coursing in them.

On they marched and fought...
alongside Lafayette and their French allies
they besieged the British at Yorktown,
and at last on October 19, 1781,
British General Cornwallis
was forced to concede the battle
and surrendered his sword to
the indomitable American hero—
General George Washington.

But what of the fifty-six patriots
who signed the fabled
Declaration of Independence...
what had it cost them—personally?

Nine fought with the Continental Army
and died from wounds and hardships suffered in the war;
Two lost their soldier sons who died in combat;
Five were captured by the British,
tortured and died in captivity;
Likewise, one lost his wife when she died,
after brutal incarceration by the British;
Twelve had their lovely homes burned to the ground
and lost all their possessions;
and some died penniless and broke...

All of this happened to them,
because they united believed as
John Adams had said,
"…there's a Divinity which shapes our ends…
Sir, before God, I believe the hour is come.
My judgment approves this measure,
and my whole heart is in it.
All that I have,
and all that I am,
and all that I hope,
in this life,
I am now ready here to stake upon it;
and I leave off as I begun,
that live or die,
survive or perish,
I am for the Declaration.
It is my living sentiment,
and by the blessing of God
it shall be my dying sentiment,
Independence now,
and Independence for ever."

These fifty-six signers of the Declaration of Independence
exemplified the spirit of sacrifice—
having lost all or nearly all they possessed,
including some their very lives—
but not one of them ever lost their sacred honor!

Praise be to the God of Abraham,
that in this last dispensation of time
he raised up such men of faith and valor,
and inspired them in the fullness of times
to lay the eternal foundations of glorious liberty,
then, now and forever.

The Circus Is Coming to Town

"The Circus is coming…"
"The Circus is coming…"
several local folks yelled.
"The Circus is coming to town
and it's the grandest show around!"
So declared a loud speaker atop a passing promotion vehicle
as the circus train pulled slowly into our old station.

P.T. Barnum once said it,
so you know it must be true.
"Imagination is the elixir of life," said he,
"and the Circus is its magic brew."

Inside the giant Circus tent
just waiting for you
to be seated and then begins
to cast a spell on you
is the Big Top Circus…
as you gaze upon a cornucopia
of Circus sights, sounds and smells.

The calliope is playing
a magic Circus tune,
the lights are dimmed…
the spotlight silhouettes a robust and regal figure—
the ringmaster who is quite a dashing sight—
in top hat, coat and tails.

In the most notable demeanor,
he gestures to the audience,
"The Greatest Show on Earth is about to begin!"
In deepest baritone—

he announces to the crowd,
all the acts as they are spotlighted
in three rings before us and we see:

Sequined costumed bareback riders—
doing acrobatic jumps
with a bounding canine hurtling between horses
and jumping through hoops,
that one deftly standing rider holds,
while somehow precariously balancing
upon a prancing white steed...

Daring motorcyclists—
gunning their motors and accelerating,
madcaply racing revolutions round and round
inside a metal sphere...first one, then two, then three.
"Hey, I'm getting dizzy just watching them.
How do they do it?"

Fearless lion tamer—
with his snapping whip raised above his head,
coaxing snarling beasts
to perch upon a wooden chair...
Oh my, everywhere one looks—
lions, tigers and bears!

The Ringmaster cranes his neck
and declares, "Now it's time for aerial wizardry
as never seen before,
high above the safety nets!"
As he points with his baton
way up above your heads,
"Look up!" he exclaims. "There are feats of daring do!"
A performer is balancing on a narrow wire
and trapeze artists in brightly colored tights,
striving to land a triple
are doing somersaults in midair!

And thirty minutes later
an animated fan declares,
"Holy Moses Marty, this is quite a show!"
With that, it's time to take a collective breath
as the aerial performers safe and sound,
descend to the Circus floor below…

Time to eat some cotton candy
and mustard dogs too—
time to watch the Circus clowns cavorting
in tiny cars, walking on stilts
and waving hello to you.

Time to watch amazed as performing dogs
run and jump over clowns in silly routines
that make us cheer and laugh,
providing happy memories
for endless days to come.

Now, before you know it,
two hours have delightfully passed
and the Circus fanfare plays…
announcing the grand finale,
the traditional close to every Circus show—
the "Majestic Circus Procession!"

All the combined Circus acts
in full costumed regalia,
are passing in review.
The most colorful of promenades you'll see anywhere,
are marching around the rings to soaring orchestral strains
and the ascending applause of appreciative folks,
whose children squirm and giggle with delight—
at the wealth of amazing sights…
under the Big Top's brightly colored lights.

And still this joyful procession passes in review…
with festooned performers in feathery plumage,
high minded hats and elaborate headdresses,
and sparkly bangles, beads and such…
riding in gaily decorated floats
and Circus carriages with proud strutting horses
leading the way.
Then come those show stoppers—
the favorite of all—those massive,
ponderous pachyderms,
curiously connected head and trunk
to swaying elephant's tails.

Oh, those famed impresarios,
what a grandiose exhibition
of talent, color and dramatic flair…
Messers: Barnum, Bailey and Ringling Brothers
have concocted to the delight
of the child in each of us,
from age three to ninety-three or more.

Oh yes, just one other thing,
I forgot to mention how much I love…
the balloons fashioned into animals by clowns
and the lizard that changes colors,
a chameleon isn't it—and of course,
the collectible programs, coloring books
and stuffed animals sold by vendors.
They're all elements of the captivating magic
that is "The Greatest Show on Earth!"

Like caramel corn, candy apples and cotton candy,
it's all part of the wonderful world of make believe—
as P.T. Barnum said, "Imagination is the elixir of life"
and the Circus is its magic brew.

It's the reason we still become excited,
whenever we hear the famous words:

"The Circus is coming..."
"The Circus is coming..."
"The Circus is coming to town
and it's the grandest show around!"

Soddy Daisy, Tennessee

In Soddy Daisy, Tennessee
the livin' is easy
and the pace of life,
well, I guess you could say,
that it was best suited
for those that were decidedly lazy.

Maybe my use of the term lazy,
is just a trifle too harsh.
I'll allow that we have a few folks,
that be residin' here,
with the gumption to usually rise early.
Yet, for the life of me I don't know why.
Good golly, by George (that's my name)
what's the hurry, I often exclaim.
Now for me, I rarely open an eye before it's even nine
or better yet ten,
now, that's the time to rise and shine.

Now for the life of me,
I can't figure what anyone would do,
fixin' themselves to get goin'
before the rest of us can barely see,
or hear farmer Charlie's aged rooster crow at eleven;
and surely not me,
before the pleasin' aroma of Aunt Tillie's
bacon and beans wafts through the air,
and fillin' my nostrils, awakened I be!

Just between you and me,
industry can plainly be left
to those that feel the compulsive need,
for constant commotion as if they were some…
well, some fandangled hummin' bird or busy bee.

It just doesn't make a bit of difference to me
if you stand, sit or sleep till three,
as long as by day's end
you've rendered some sort of kindness,
to some ol' folk residin' here,
in Soddy Daisy, Tennessee.

Take for example, yesterday in Central Park.
I spied ol' Mildred tackin' to a weepin' willow tree,
a notice for any and all to see.
"Y'all come to the local bazaar every Tuesday,
at the corner of Main Street and Maple
is the place in which we casually meet —
the nostalgic Cinema Rialto."

"Surely y'all recall how we once shared
flickering moments in the darkened film cathedral
while life's spectacle played-out on the silver screen.
Do you recall those lusty leading men —
Power, Tracy and Gable,
and as well those stylish starlets too —
Loy, Lamarr and Colbert,
who dashingly and romantically performed their inimitable magic
in our historic art deco movie palace of dreams?"
"Sponsored by we ladies with civic pride,
members of Wanda's Ladies Club, say heartily to you,
Now, don't be left out — see ya at 2 p.m. — at the fabled
Rialto!"

Yes, I know,
everywhere one looks in our ol' town,
from Granny's Memories Store,
to the Daughters of the Civil War,

tradition is all quite pervasive and what's more,
yesterday I was readin' the *Daisy Gazette*
and the banner declared,
"Fired by Truman, MacArthur arrives home!"

If I were an outsider I'd certainly question
whether the editor was kiddin'
or was this headline a revealin' clue,
to a slower pace of life that most of us bemuse.
Because, ya see, in Soddy Daisy, Tennessee
we're all part recluse.

Those of us abidin' here in timeless harmony,
well, we gladly admit we're quite fortunate
to be residin' here where the livin' is easy
and the enchantin' past is always present...
where life's values remain constant,
apart from the trendy, turbulent outside world.
Here we enjoy the simple timeless pleasures
often taken for granted in faraway places.
However, all good things remain evergreen,
here in remarkably cordial and thoughtful—
Soddy Daisy, Tennessee.

Billy Bucks: The Boy Who Ate Raspberry Jellies

Billy and I were close childhood friends,
mainly because we were also cousins.
My name is Josie,
and I must truthfully exclaim,
that, although I did love him,
Billy had to assuredly be,
the unrivaled rogue of spoiledness!
For several years in the mid-fifties you see,
we lived across the street
from each other,
and just a hop, skip and jump,
to Denny's Big Donuts—and cream filled,
or my personal favorites,
raspberry jellies—the choicest of glazed donuts!

During the summer months,
we spent so much time together,
nearly every day we joyfully pursued,
typical boyhood (I was a tomboy) pleasures.

Armies at War

We would often start,
by playing "Armies at War"
and out we'd haul,
each our own toy militaria collection.
Each of us possessed Dinky Toy planes and tanks and assorted
plastic soldiers and other miniature scale weapons
of World War II.

After several hours of heated combat,
it was time to move on.
But not before taking stock of the vast carnage
of mock death and destruction,
of plastic soldiers toting Tommy Guns, Grenades and Bazookas,
and toppled Tanks and crashed Silver Planes too,
laying strewn across the imaginary battlefield,
masquerading as a tiny Sahara,
during the European theater of conflict
of World War II.

And all of this,
imagined by two youthful minds,
at play and war,
in Billy's four by four backyard box,
of playful sand and mystic lore.

Amazing isn't it,
when you consider that all this chaotic destruction
will be repaired in time,
to imaginatively clash again on the morrow.
Not so much for victory or liberty did we contest,
as for supremacy of Billy and Josie's
creative new worlds of adventures.
Fighting it out, we bravely soldiered on,
slugging it out between imaginary forces
of Allied and Axis
toy soldiers, tanks and planes,
during the harrowing conflict
Of World War II!

After several hours of exhausting combat…

Dueling Marbles

It was time to ease our way toward lunch,
with a more comforting, gentile game,
known to us as simply,
"Dueling Marbles!"

As with most games featuring marbles,
the applicable rules we made ourselves.
The "Game" consisted of only two "HotShot" players, I
suppose you know to whom I'm modestly referring?
The players then placed nine marbles each into the center ring,
three each from the Exquisite class,
the Desirable class, and lastly,
the Unremarkable class.

The process of negotiating the suitability of each marble,
by class distinction was a game unto its self.
Once this sticky issue had been settled to mutual satisfaction,
it was time to set aside our treasured marblebox,
or weathered draw-string bag,
and unlimber our most trusty,
bull's-eye, marble-shooting finger!

Both of us being quite intent on winning
the entire spherical stache of the other,
even their unremarkable class,
got right down to the right fine art of
marbling.

Before the dust had settled,
from several dozen furious finger flippings,
and the smacking sound of colliding shooters and targets,
now careening away in a marblelistic blur,

Billy Bucks' marbles were now mine.
And fortuitously, so also
were my original nine as well as my special,
"Big Bertha—
The Heavyweight Queen of Shooters!"

Now, lest I deceive you into thinking,
I was the Annie Oakley of marble shooting,
let me judiciously say,
my cousin Billy was just seven,
while I was pushing the superior age of eleven.

However, it truly mattered little,
that I had triumphed, because before long,
cousin Billy would break into his well rehearsed song,
"Auntie Ellen, Josie has taken all my marbles!"
You guessed it,
in the twinkling of an eye,
the little brat's marbles were magically his again,
and to compensate for my transgression,
so was my most prized "Big Bertha."
What was I gonna do?
Who could I appeal to?
Either Billy won fair and square (rarely),
or I lost on appeal (mostly).
There just weren't other options,
according to angelic Billy,
or my doting (on Billy),
believing Mother!

Denny's Big Donuts

As if that miscarriage of justice was not enough,
Mom firmly suggested (Ha),
I take Billy by the hand and accompany him,
to Denny's Big Donuts.
"Take a dollar from your Piggy Bank," she said,
"and get you each a carton of milk,
and one each of your favorite flavored Big Donuts."

When we arrived I could almost taste my very favorite,
the raspberry jelly-filled glazed donut.
Yet, following my mom's directions to the letter,
I let Billy choose first, fully expecting him to select, as he was
prone to do, the cream filled donut.
But not on my life was anything going right that contrary day,
as I astonishingly heard my capricious cousin Billy,
unhesitatingly declare,
"Give me that last one there,
yeah,
the 'raspberry jellies' one."

In Your Face!

Oh, I guess, it wasn't the most lady-like thing to have done,
but I hadn't outgrown all my tomboyishness yet,
and it felt indescribably good as my fingers probed every
crevice of his contorted, freckled-face and pumpkin colored hair,
with the joyfully squished "raspberry jellies,"
the choicest of glazed donuts!

Around and around my nimble fingers raced,
until every square inch of his freckled-face,
including the eyes, ears, nose and chin were thoroughly
traced,

196

in red jellyish gooh and the sticky remains of
one of Denny's choicest glazed donuts!
Thank you, oh, thank you,
Denny's Big Donuts.

Epilogue

I've never enjoyed one of your donuts more, before or since,
that day long ago,
before I became too old to be bold,
and
too set in my ways to be playfully spontaneous!

Encounter with Tonga

It was the summer of 1978. I was attending a nostalgia and collectibles Show at the Civic Auditorium in my home town of Glendale, California. I had scarcely entered the main exhibit hall when I saw a strikingly attractive lady who looked vaguely familiar. I thought I knew her from somewhere, but I couldn't quite recall where. She was sitting in her corner booth at the head of the main aisle. As I approached her table, I saw some photos with a sign which read, "Special Guest Nina Bara—Tonga of *SPACE PATROL*."

Immediately my mind was flooded with pleasant memories from my childhood in Los Angeles from 1951 through 1953. I fondly recalled watching *Space Patrol* episodes on television every Saturday morning. Like many pre-teens, I had a crush on Tonga, the femme fatale who was my favorite character of this early groundbreaking space opera.

The rest of the competent cast was led by the unflappable Commander Buzz Corry (Ed Kemmer). Then there was the comic relief provided by Cadet Happy (Lynn Osborn) with his oft repeated refrain, "Smokin' rockets, Commander." Of course, no show in its right mind would be without a blonde heroine, in this case her name was Carol (Virginia Hewitt), the commander's girlfriend. Rounding out the cast was the robust Major Robbie Robertson (Ken Mayer), Security Chief of the United Planets.

In addition to the regular cast were several frequent visitors. The villainous Prince Bacarrati was played by Bela Kovacs who eventually became assistant producer of *Space Patrol*. Another nemesis was the shadowy Agent X, played by Norman Jolley whose main job was to crank out the many required scripts as the show's beleaguered writer. Also, the regular show announcer, Jack Narz, sometimes appeared as a space cadet.

I could not resist approaching Ms Bara to introduce myself and to tell her how much I had enjoyed *Space Patrol*. It was wonderful to meet her after all those years. She was remarkably warm and genuinely pleased that the show had a positive impact on me as a youngster.

Space Patrol was produced during the earliest years of television, when there was a great deal of experimentation in the medium. This early entry into broadcast science fiction had a very loyal following. Much of this rabid popularity, was due in no small part to the crew and cast's dedication. They genuinely enjoyed what they were doing, and the unique chemistry that grew between actors, writer, director and producers over time. This bond of trust helped foster working together as a "family." Without this special relationship, the confidence to experiment would have been missing, and hence, so too would much of the show's unique style and charm.

Space Patrol was born in an era of optimism and great expectations regarding the future of space exploration. Previous decades of science fiction media had been dominated by such remarkably popular characters as Flash Gordon and Buck Rogers. As the fifties and the new medium of television arrived, the opportunities for new adventure stories and heroes of the space-ways were presented.

The two most popular new space genre shows to step forward to fill this void were *Space Patrol* and Tom Corbett Space Cadet. They were wonderful shows that conveyed timeless values mixed with optimism to a youthful audience hungry for new heroes facing new challenges.

Space Patrol first rocketed into the public's consciousness in the fall of 1950 and quickly attracted a substantial nationwide audience on the American Broadcasting Co. network. It was the brainchild of Mike Mosher who first conceived the show during his military service in the Second World War. The show's director, Dik Darley, was young and talented and made a significant contribution to the development and success of *Space Patrol*. The show remained popular through its final season in 1955. The reason it ended then was not due to falling ratings, but failed negotiations by ABC to acquire equity in *Space Patrol* from the producer.

While it ran however, it sizzled. Fan clubs abounded throughout the states, in Canada and Japan. When the cast wasn't in rehearsal or on the air, they were on the road making public appearances. They were on the front of magazine covers, licensed products filled toy store shelves and nearly everywhere else. Two of my favorite collectibles were sponsor's premiums that could only be acquired by sending in a product box top and a nominal fee. One was a cosmic smoke gun and the other a cardboard space helmet with one-way viewing eyepiece. I convinced my mom that I needed these items to truly get into the spirit of the stories.

These shows provided the young post WWII generation of Americans who anticipated the future with hope, just what they needed. They had been searching for a positive futuristic vision amid the tensions of the Korean War. In the era that immediately preceded "sputnik" and the race to the moon, *Space Patrol* gave America's youth a preview of themselves. "Smokin' Rockets," as Cadet Happy would exclaim, "We arrived just in the nick of time!"

The Duke of Ebbets

In the history of American pop culture in the twentieth century, the nickname "Duke" is remembered in high esteem for three accomplished performers in different mediums. "Duke," as applied to these three individuals, was not merely a nickname, but a title of respected status in their respective fields. It implied that as a performer, you were acclaimed by the public to be at the top level in your chosen vocation.

If you were a musician, as my father was prior to WWII or simply loved stylish music of the Big Band era and Jazz in the Thirties and Forties, then "Duke" could only refer to the elegant maestro of music, Duke Ellington. Everything about Ellington from his musicianship, to his gracious manner, sophisticated speech and attire bespoke style and grace.

In the entire history of American Cinema, no star shined brighter or longer than did the star of John Wayne. Beginning in 1939 with the film Stagecoach, which made him a star, to his last film, The Shootist, everyone knew who was referred to by the media or others when they simply invoked the name "Duke." Among the approximately two hundred films Wayne appeared in, were such classics as *The Sands of Iwo Jima, They Were Expendable, Red River, The Quiet Man, She Wore a Yellow Ribbon, The Searchers and True Grit.*

The third Duke was a major league baseball player who performed so consistently at an exceptionally high level that he was elected to the Baseball Hall of Fame in 1980. Edwin Snider was one of the best ever at his position of centerfield. Ironically, three of the greatest centerfielders in baseball history were contemporaries who all played for Major League Baseball teams in New York during the fifties.

Even New Yorkers couldn't decide among themselves, who was the superior player among the three superstars: Mickey Mantle of the Yankees, Willie Mays of the Giants or Edwin Snider of the Dodgers. All three had speed to steal bases and chase down fly balls, could throw out base runners with their powerful arms, and hit for power, average and RBIs. All three of these great players were selected to the Major League Baseball Hall of Fame.

The Brooklyn Dodgers fielded consistently competitive teams in the decades of the forties and fifties. They perennially challenged for the National League Championship and seldom finished lower than second place in their league. From 1940 to 1957 (their last season in Brooklyn) the Dodgers finished lower than third place in the National League only one time—1944 when they finished up seventh. During that eighteen year stretch they won the National League Pennant seven times: 1941, 1947, 1949, 1952, 1953, 1955 and 1956. Snider was a member of the last six of those pennant winning teams.

More often than not, they either finished second or won the National League Pennant and appeared in the World Series. The only problem was they seemed to always run into one of those feared NY Yankee juggernaut teams that would repeatedly defeat them in the Fall Classic except for that wonderful 1955 team.

Nevertheless, "Dem Bums of Flatbush" had a loyal following. They played in the smallish, economical Ebbets Field Stadium that was built in 1913 over an old garbage dump in the poor Flatbush section of the city. It was the only tract of available land of sufficient acreage that the team's owner, Charlie Ebbets could afford to purchase and still afford to construct the stadium.

Ebbets Field was a far cry from the "Palace that Ruth built"—Yankee Stadium, where such stars of the game as Lou Gerhrig, Babe Ruth and Joe DiMaggio were showcased.

However, over the decades the austere Flatbush stadium seemed to grow on the Dodgers' fans and players. Ebbets Field fit them comfortably, like an old broken-in pair of shoes does to your feet. You knew what to expect when you put them on, and the same was true when you went to see the Dodgers at Ebbets. After all, they weren't pretentious like the imperialistic Yankees. There were few if any frills, but the dogs were good and "Dem Bums" provided a thrill, laugh or heartbreak a minute. What more could you expect from a team originally dubbed the "Trolley Dodgers?"

The Dodgers in the forties had plenty of stars on their own roster, such as the power hitting first baseman, Dolph Camilli, reliable second baseman Eddie Stanky, playmaking shortstop Peewee Reese, batting champ Dixie Walker, consistently good hitting outfielder Pete Reiser and winning pitchers Whit Wyatt, Kirby Higbe, Ralph Branca and Don Newcombe.

It was into this unique environment that Edwin "Duke" Snider arrived when he joined the team for the 1947 season. He was full of raw talent but it took two years of somewhat frustrating play and diligent schooling by hitting coach George Sisler to refine Snider's raw but substantial skills.

However by the 1949 season Snider had earned a starting position in the Dodgers' outfield. It happened at just the time a number of other star players had emerged or were beginning to replace the successful but aging Dodger players of the forties.

Gil Hodges had become a power hitting fixture at first base, as was star catcher Roy Campanella behind the plate. Jackie Robinson, who joined the Dodgers at the same time as Snider, became ensconced at second base. PeeWee Reese, who had been the starting shortstop since 1940, was still working his magic at turning double plays and getting clutch hits. Alongside Snider in the outfield was the always reliable Carl Furillo who could be counted on to deliver 80 plus RBI and a .280 + batting average annually. On the pitching mound, the Dodgers could rely on veteran starters Don Newcombe, Carl Erskine, Ralph Branca and reliever Clem Labine.

In his first season as a starter for the Dodgers in 1949, the Duke hit 23 home runs with 92 RBI. It was quite an auspicious start for the young man from Los Angeles. Yet, it was only a foretaste of greater things to come in the decade of the fifties.

I started watching baseball on television in Los Angeles in 1954 when I was ten years old. One of the factors that made me a fan of the American pastime were those black and white television images of Duke leading the Dodgers to exciting victories. I can still recall scenes fifty years later of Snider robbing the great Stan Musial of an extra base hit with a running catch in centerfield to beat the Cardinals in St. Louis; or a clutch hit to defeat the always tough pitcher Lou Burdette of the Milwaukee Braves.

Everything he did on the ball field appeared effortless. When you watch a ballet, you intuitively know the male dancers have tremendous strength to perform those acrobatic jumps, twirls, catches and lifts and yet appear to do them with such grace and ease. That was the same magic spell that Duke could cast upon the fans in attendance when he played baseball. It was truly a high wire act of the uttermost skill, competence and grace.

During the four years from 1954 to 1957, when all three great NY centerfielders (Mays for the Giants, Mantle for the Yankees and Snider with the Dodgers) were starters for their respective teams, Duke lead the way with most home runs and RBI. He also led all Major League players for total home runs hit during the decade of the fifties with 326 round trippers.

In the Brooklyn Dodgers' most memorable season in 1955, when Duke led the team to the World Championship, he was named that season's Most Outstanding Player by The Sporting News.

Perhaps, that which most set him apart from the other extremely talented players of his day in my estimation had little to do with physical skill and everything to do with character. He always handled himself in an appropriate fashion on and off the field. Duke epitomized the word dignity.

Another athlete that comes to mind in that regard was Ernie Davis, the Heisman Trophy winning running back from Syracuse University; and of course, Duke's teammate, Jackie Robinson was not wanting in that capacity either.

With his premature graying hair, handsome features and pleasant demeanor, he had the aura of a compassionate, quiet leader of men like General Omar Bradley was in WWII. He was as different from his effervescent NY Giants rival, Willie "The Say Hey Kid" Mays, as was General Bradley from his contemporary, "The Hell on Wheels" General George Patton. Both centerfielders, as well as both generals excelled in their positions.

It was a preference of style that drew me to Duke. It was so refreshing to observe someone so talented and graceful on the field, be so consistently gracious, dignified and humble off it. That's not to slight Mays or Mantle in any way. It's just that Snider radiated an exceptional quality of gentile civility that was palpable.

Baseball, more than any other sport, is a game measured by statistics. However, there is one element of the game that cannot be quantified by any certifiable standard beyond personal judgment, and that is character. In that regard, Snider impressed me more than any other player of his time or since.

Five decades have passed since that marvelous 1955 season. As I observe the callous world of professional sports today, I can't help but think how nice it would be for young people to once again witness the positive example of Duke Snider. True greatness was routinely on display in '55 by one of the finest "Boys of Summer" to ever play the game, one Edwin "Duke" Snider. On or off the field, the Duke of Ebbets hit the ball out of the park!

Way out in Front

The Story of a Boy and His Hero

I sat there, drinking it all in. No, I don't mean the Coke my mom was holding for me while I feverishly devoured a hot dog with both hands. I am referring to the colorful atmosphere and excitement of the event. It was November 1948, on a rather cool and blustery night in San Diego, CA. My parents and I were celebrating my fourth birthday by attending the midget races at cozy Balboa Stadium.

The cramped little stadium was shaped like a bowl and was an ideal setting for the "Mighty Midgets" that raced in similar facilities throughout California three or four nights a week. No matter where you sat, you were on top of the action.

Mom sat on one side of me, and Dad on the other. I guess they wanted to ensure that if I got excited, and madly waved my hot dog, I wouldn't get mustard and relish on a perfect stranger. They knew all too well my lively nature and propensity for excitability.

Somehow, tonight's sights, sounds and smells overwhelmed me. I was actually quiet as I sat transfixed by the snarling of fine-tuned "Offy" racing engines being revved, the unmistakable smell of midget fuel and the myriad of colors reflected by the stadium lights off the brightly painted little cars.

The main event was about to begin. The drivers had just completed the parade lap and now were bracing themselves for the start of the feature race. You could feel the energy of 18 powerful engines straining to be unleashed. Just as they rounded the final turn and headed for the green flag, my mom informed me, "Watch the car on the outside of the last row—that's Vuky!

Sure enough, by the time those feisty drivers in their roaring midget cars had sped past the starter waving the green flag energetically, shot through the first turn and exited the second turn, Billy was on the move. He had already passed three competitors in less than half a lap! At the completion of the tenth lap, Billy had fought his way through the field and was now in third place. He passed cars in the turns by knifing under them while in a controlled slide or blasted by them on the short straights. It didn't seem to matter to Billy Vukovich where he encountered another midget, he was going by.

It's no wonder that many in attendance called him "The Mad Russian" or "The Fresno Flash." His driving style was inimitable. He could put that midget racer anywhere he wanted to on a dirt track and do it without losing momentum. He drove with unmatched passion. You would have thought he was Errol Flynn, leading "The Charge of the Light Brigade" at Sebastopol. That is what really set him apart from all other drivers—his competitive fire.

Race drivers by nature are competitive individuals, but Billy was a cut above everyone else in that department. Even in the slam-bang world of open wheel auto racing, Billy was without peer. If Billy was in a race, he was in it to win!

Billy took the lead on the twelfth lap and pulled away. By lap fifteen, he was way out in front by half a lap and roared on to a decisive victory. Billy was never content to just win; he wanted to destroy the competition. Billy only knew one way to drive, which was with the gas pedal pressed all the way to the floor.

At the end of the post race activities, fans were permitted to go down to the infield and meet the drivers, which we did. Dad had me on his shoulders and headed straight to Billy's pit. I don't recall what was said, but the next thing I knew I was being passed to the strong grip of someone who gently sat me in the driver's seat of the winning car. He leaned over and quietly explained a few things to me about the cockpit of his dirt splattered midget. As he did so, I noticed the outline where his driver's goggles had been. He hadn't even had time to wipe the racing grime off his face.

That was it. It was all over in less than five minutes, and he was gone. But the indelible impression of his gentle strength and quiet warmth will forever remain with me—as will the sight of him running at the head of the pack—"Way Out In Front!"

Epilogue

Although, I was stunned when I received the news of Vuky's tragic accident and death at the 1955 Indianapolis 500, the details of the circumstances surrounding the demise of the Fresno Flash certainly did not. As I've pointed out, when Billy climbed into the cockpit of a race car, he was there for only one purpose—to win.

Once he was strapped into his office, he became focused beyond what we mere mortals can understand. He raced his racing car much the same as he operated his corner service station in Fresno, he was all business. Vuky's driving style was like General George Patton driving a Sherman tank through the German Panzers at the "Battle of the Bulge" to relieve the "Battered Bastards of Bastonge." It was straight forward and without frills.

Billy simply didn't have time for frills. He was out to win and to do it by the widest margin possible. It was true that he was a virtuoso driver, the equal of any racing chauffer who ever strapped on a helmet and goggles, including his Argentinean contemporary, the famed Juan Manuel Fangio of the Formula One circuits in Europe. Like the champion thoroughbred Man of War, once Billy got in front, the race was over.

Come the month of May 1955, Billy and his team had once again returned to the scene of his greatest triumphs—Indianapolis Motor Speedway in the little town of Speedway, Indiana. In many ways it was similar to Billy's hometown of Fresno, California.

After several frustrating years at Indy, trying to win the world's most prestigious auto race, Billy had broken through at the "brickyard" in 1953 to win his first "500 Championship." The previous year, 1952, had almost seen him accomplish the feat. The "Mad Russian" as some referred to him, had dominated nearly the entire race and had a substantial lead until a small steering part broke just eight laps from the checkered flag. Billy had to bring his car to a sliding stop against the outside wall within spitting distance of a masterful triumph.

Billy was outraged, and unloaded a string of colorful invectives to anyone within earshot of his garage in "Gasoline Alley" following the race. Perhaps it wouldn't have been such a crushing defeat, had he not lead the eventual winner by over a mile when he crashed. But, those are the types of things that often happen to those seeking to challenge the fates of the speedway.

1954 saw Billy accomplish a rare second consecutive 500 victory that had been previously done only twice. Many race officials, broadcasters, reporters and fans were predicting a precedent setting third consecutive victory for Billy in 1955. It had never been done before, but if anyone could, Billy was the man.

It was somewhat ironic, but Billy had mentioned to his wife that he was not all that excited about participating in the '55 race. Over the last half decade, he had elected to drive in fewer and fewer races. He simply had lost his passion for the grind of driving on either the west coast or national midget or big car circuits. His family and his business interests were more important and frankly he had nothing left to prove in auto racing.

Once, however, as the 1955 race day pageantries drew inexorably to a close, and he was again securely harnessed into his sleek Kurtis constructed, Offenhauser powered number 4 roadster, Billy's competitive fires burned as brightly as ever. His fiercest competitor was the hard charging Jack McGrath. Sure enough, McGrath took the lead from the start and by the second lap Billy had worked his way to second from his fifth starting spot. On the fourth lap Billy caught McGrath and passed him for the first time.

Then began one of the toughest two driver battles in speedway history. Back and forth they went, swapping the lead over the next 21 laps. Billy's daring pass of McGrath in the first turn on lap 16 where he put all four wheels of his "Hopkins Special" below the white line was considered by many speedway old timers as the most amazing driving maneuver ever at the "Brickyard." McGrath got the lead back one final time on lap 25.

Finally, Billy, anxious to put his prime contender behind him, roared up on McGrath's tail and rocketed past him on the backstretch of lap 27. He was never to be passed on the track again. His metallic blue and orange KK500C roadster shot past the determined McGrath and into the lead for good, or so many imagined. Many also imagined this might just be the most dominate display of speedway artistry they had witnessed. His legion of fans knew that once Billy wrested the lead from McGrath, there would be no one else to stop him from entering Victory Lane for the third consecutive time.

McGrath's attempts to hold off Billy had caused his own Kurtis roadster which had been showing puffs of exhaust smoke from early in the race, to finally break and he pulled into the pits on lap 54, his car and race finished.

Billy was driving like a man possessed, passing car after car, until only seven other competitors remained on the same lap with him. Billy zoomed past the start finish line completing lap 56 and dove into turn one of lap 57. He traversed the short chute between the first and second turns and emerged from turn two, gunning his engine to extend his impressive lead. All he had on his mind at this moment, was steadily pulling away from the other drivers, and wining the race so he could return to his family and home that much sooner.

It would have been a wonderful scenario, but unfortunately, as so often occurs with fate, it didn't work out that way. A three car tangle was precipitated when Rodger Ward spun after exiting turn two, hitting the outside wall and sliding several hundred yards, rolling twice and coming to a stop upright and facing oncoming cars including those of Al Keller, Johnny Boyd and Billy who were running closely in that order.

In quick succession, Keller turned hard left for the infield, locked his brakes on the edge of the infield grass, lost control and veered sharply right directly into the path of Boyd. In a blur, he collected Boyd and pushed him to the right. This clogged the back straight with wrecked and spinning cars just as Billy was beginning an evasive initial move left to avoid Ward's crashing car further down the backstretch. Then, out of his field of vision to the immediate left came the unexpected threat of Keller's and Boyd's runaway cars. He had but a heartbeat to make a life or death decision on where to steer the car. He made a split-second instinctive reaction to turn right at the last moment—to save his racecar and life…maybe he could barely squeeze his #4 through the crashing cars before the escape window closed…and why not? He had led a charmed life, this son of a hard working Yugoslavian immigrant family.

This time Billy, in spite of his enormous talent, simply ran out of time and space. His path was abruptly blocked by the careening car of Boyd that was headed toward the outside wall after being struck by an out of control Keller. Billy ran over the left rear wheel of Boyd's car in the crazy melee. The beautiful Kurtis built and Lindsey Hopkins owned racing machine was instantly launched skyward, clearing the retaining wall just beyond the pedestrian bridge. The wildly gyrating roadster began a several hundred yard mad ricocheting flight. Flipping end over end, car number 4 bounced off three parked vehicles, clipped a power pole and crashed to earth upside down, exploding in flames on a service road just beyond the backstretch retaining wall.

The officials slowed the race as a precaution, as they always did when there had been a serious racing accident. Emergency personnel raced to the scene of the crash to see what assistance, if any could be offered one of the world's greatest drivers. A hushed silence fell over millions of spectators not only at the speedway, but around the world who were following the race on syndicated radio.

A small foreboding plume of smoke hung high in the sky, marking the spot where Billy's once beautiful roadster had plummeted to earth. Those who were on the front straight, including spectators, race officials, media, pit crews and even some drivers, were too removed from the accident scene to know for some time what had happened.

As the remaining drivers slowed and came into or exited the pits, anxious fans and Billy's pit crew including Frank Coon and Jim Travers, kept searching for their favorite driver in the sleek, low slung blue and orange number four. They craned their necks, staring anxiously up the main straight to turn four, hoping against fading hope to see their hero's car appear in the distance. Some questioned the air, "Where's Vuky?" "Did I miss him go by?" "Did anyone see or hear anything about Vuky in car number four?"

Others mumbled softly, almost in the attitude of prayer, "Where's Billy, what's become of Billy?" Then, as long minutes passed, word of mouth was starting to spread around the two and one half mile oval as details were coming to light about who was involved. In what seemed like an eternity but was probably less than an hour, there came across the vast speedway radio network the official word.

The somber voice of race broadcaster Sid Collins, almost devoid of emotion, gave the news so many anticipated, yet hated to hear. The announcer who had previously informed all listeners of the cars and drivers involved in the incident, regretfully announced, "Fans, we have some very, very disheartening news to relate to you…Bill Vukovich, three time winner of the 500 mile race, almost, trying for his third consecutive today, was trapped in his car in the accident on the backstretch and has been injured fatally…!"

Bang! Like a balloon popping in front of your face, you're immediately disoriented. Slowly getting hold of your senses, you ask what happened and is this all of the explanation? Just as simple as that, many folks could not or would not believe what they had just heard.

Many a pair of eyes welled up with tears, and not just fans, but tough old mechanics, cynical reporters and even other hardened drivers. They all found something special to be cherished in this honorable man. Yes, he was quiet, sometimes moody and the fiercest competitor you would ever encounter on a track. But Billy was also honest, hard working, devoted to his family and very loyal to the friends he knew.

Fortunately, for Billy and his family, he had died instantly from a skull fracture suffered either during the wild gyrations of the car while cart-wheeling through the air or upon its forceful impact with the ground upside down.

"Vuky," as he was affectionately called by nearly everyone who loved and admired him, was gone. However, I don't think he will

212

ever be forgotten as long as there is at least one race fan alive that is old enough to remember the one and only true "King of American Open-Wheel Auto Racing!"

A New Vision
of Classic
Entertainment

The Golden Age of the Studio Era

Once upon a time, there was a glorious world of motion picture entertainment produced at magnificent dream factories known as the studio lots of Metro Goldwyn Mayer, Twentieth Century Fox, Warner Brothers, Columbia, Paramount, Universal, RKO, and Republic.

These were times of soaring imagination and unparalleled craftsmanship. It came to be known as "the Golden Age of Hollywood Cinema." I equate the general beginning of this era with Columbia's release of *It Happened One Night* in 1934 and the approximate end of this era with MGM's release of *Ben Hur* in 1959.

Obviously, there were a number of landmark films produced earlier during the silent film era, *The Birth of a Nation* in 1915 and *Intolerance* in 1916 to name two. Then, the release of *The Jazz Singer* in 1927 heralded the passing of the "silents" and ushered in the "talkies." This advancement in motion picture technology set the stage for the advent of the "Golden Age."

Similarly, there have been a number of quality films released since 1959. Meredith Wilson's *The Music Man* in 1961, Lerner and Loewe's *My Fair Lady* in 1964, and Rogers and Hammerstein's *The Sound of Music* in 1965 are all exceptional films. However, since 1970 feature film production has been marked by a glut of "R" rated and big budget special effects films. Only a relative handful of quality films suitable for viewing by the entire family (excluding animated films) have been produced during the past four decades.

The major studios during the "Golden Age" were known for their powerful top executives such as Louis B. Mayer, Harry Cohn, Jack Warner and Darryl F. Zanuck. The films their studios released featured glamorous stars: Clark Gable, Spencer Tracy, Fred Astaire, Jimmy Stewart, James Cagney, John Wayne, Gary Cooper, Cary Grant, Bing Crosby, Robert Taylor, Tyrone Power, Errol Flynn, Gregory Peck, Humphrey Bogart, Burt Lancaster, Kirk Douglas, William Holden, Gene Kelly, Rock Hudson, Claudette Colbert, Barbara Stanwyck, Olivia de Havilland, Myrna Loy,

Katherine Hepburn, Lucille Ball, Greer Garson, Ginger Rogers, Judy Garland, Betty Grable, Lana Turner, June Allyson, Deborah Kerr, Esther Williams, Ava Gardner, Jane Powell and Elizabeth Taylor, to name but a few.

Most of all, these were times of collaborative genius where individuals of diverse talents worked together to create magic on the silver screen. There were directors: Cecil B. DeMille, John Ford, Frank Capra, Victor Fleming, William Wyler, Michael Curtiz, George Stevens, Robert Wise, Vincente Minnelli; composers: Max Steiner, Bernard Herrmann, Erich Wolfgang Korngold, Franz Waxman, Alfred Newman, Dimitri Tiomkin; art directors: Cedric Gibbons, William Cameron Menzies, Hal Pereira, Lyle Wheeler; screenwriters: Robert Sherwood, Ben Hecht, Ernest Lehman; cinematographers: James Wong Howe, Gregg Towland, Robert Surtees; special effects: Arnold Gillespie; Warren Newcombe; Ray Harryhausen; George Pal; color consultant: Natalie Kalmus; choreographers: Busby Berkeley, Charles Walters, Hermes Pan, Michael Kidd; costume designers: Helen Rose, Walter Plunkett, Edith Head, Irene Sharaff; makeup and hair: William Tuttle; Sydney Guilaroff, and the Westmore brothers, among many, many others who worked tirelessly behind the cameras to contribute their art to the collaborative magic of film production.

It was an era that encompassed three decades (the thirties, forties and fifties). It was also governed creatively by a production code that was put into effect in 1934 and established standards for story content and production values. The production code was administered by Will Hays and had the effect of heightening creativity and not limiting it as some have declared. It merely required that producers and talent alike subscribe to a higher standard of art and artistic expression. In that process the very finest examples of the cinematic art were elicited from filmmakers.

General principles of the code required that "No picture shall be produced which will lower the standards of those who see it. Hence, the sympathy of the audience should never be thrown to the side of crime, wrongdoing, evil or sin." Sadly, by 1966, Supreme Court decisions concerning obscenity and the pressure of civil liberty groups ultimately brought an end to the code which sought to uphold moral decency and good taste.

However, the death of the production code was merely the last act of an unfolding tragedy. This golden age of motion picture production and the studio system which fostered it, began to unwind in 1951 when Louis B. Mayer was forced out as the head of MGM. Mayer was a staunch conservative, and the typical MGM film largely reflected his belief in wholesome entertainment and his moral convictions regarding virtue, patriotism and family life.

A perfect example of a "Mayer film," is the Andy Hardy film series that featured Mickey Rooney, one of the most diversely talented performers in film history. One of Mr. Mayer's proudest moments occurred in 1942 when the series was awarded a special Oscar "for its achievement in representing the American Way of Life."

What followed the departure of Mayer from MGM and indeed eventually permeated all the studios was a production philosophy that sentimentality and traditional idealism should be played down, if not abandoned altogether. It was replaced by the "realism of the streets" school of movie making, which had originated in New York. This gritty, cynical and pessimistic view of life ushered in the role of the anti-hero, vulgar language, nudity, graphic violence and sex, and story themes that assaulted traditional values.

It was all done in the name of corporate profit by individuals sadly lacking any vision of the importance of traditional Judeo-Christian spiritual ideals or commitment to their related classic Western values in maintaining a healthy society. Regrettably, many industry executives failed to heed the Savior's admonition: "For what is a man profited, if he shall gain the whole world, and lose his own soul?" (Matthew 16:26).

Alas, the golden age, which produced the greatest of all films, is no more. Just consider some of them: *It Happened One Night*, 1934; *Mutiny on the Bounty*, 1935; *Captain Blood*, 1935; *Mr. Deeds Goes to Town*, 1936; *Swing Time*, 1936; *Lost Horizon*, 1937; *The Adventures of Robin Hood*, 1938; *Boy's Town*, 1938; *Gone with the Wind*, 1939; *The*

Wizard of Oz, 1939; *Mr. Smith Goes To Washington*, 1939; *Stagecoach*, 1939; *The Philadelphia Story*, 1940; *Foreign Correspondent*, 1940; *Sergeant York*, 1941; *The Maltese Falcon*, 1941; *King's Row*, 1942; *Yankee Doodle Dandy*, 1942; *Casablanca*, 1943; *The More the Merrier*, 1943; *Meet Me in St. Louis*, 1944; *Going My Way*, 1944; *Since You Went Away*, 1944; *The Bells of St. Mary's*, 1945; *The Best Years of Our Lives*, 1946; *It's a Wonderful Life*, 1946; *Mr. Deeds Goes To Town*, 1946; *The Razor's Edge*, 1946; *The Bishop's Wife*, 1947; *Miracle on 34th Street*, 1947; *Easter Parade*, 1948; *Romance on the High Seas*, 1948; *12 O'Clock High*, 1949; *Born Yesterday*, 1950; *King Solomon's Mines*, 1950; *The African Queen*, 1951; *The Day the Earth Stood Still*, 1951; *Singin' in the Rain*, 1951; *High Noon*, 1952; *The Quiet Man*, 1952; *The Greatest Show on Earth*, 1952; *Shane*, 1953; *Roman Holiday*, 1953; *Seven Brides for Seven Brothers*, 1954; *The Cain Mutiny*, 1954; *The Country Girl*, 1954; *Picnic*, 1955; *Love Is a Many-Splendored Thing*, 1955; *Mister Roberts*, 1955; *The Ten Commandments*, 1956; *Around the World in Eighty Days*, 1956; *Giant*, 1956; *The King And I*, 1956; *Raintree County*, 1957; *Funny Facy*, 1957; *Gigi*, 1958; *The Big Country*, 1958; *Ben Hur*, 1959; *North by Northwest*, 1959; and *Pillow Talk*, 1959 as examples of many marvelous motion pictures produced during this era which made us laugh, cry, inspired and thrilled us.

When high ideals and absolute truths fade from view in modern entertainment, it is a clarion call to change or suffer the inevitable consequences. How long can we as a society prostrate ourselves in the cultural gutter, drinking in the images and messages of humanistic depravity and not become terminally ill as to our national spirit?

We should have given heed then and even more so today to the admonition of Louis B. Mayer, when he professed, "Make it big, do it right, give it class!"

A Voyage Toward Perfection

No individual, industry or institution in our present-day society or global economy exists as an island unto itself, completely removed from all others. All organized endeavor of modern man exists in a sea of plasmic data and dynamic change. No matter how diverse or seemingly disparate the purposes and conventions of these man-made islands of endeavor are, they share a common bond.

It is a sea of rippling expectations, hopes, dreams and energies which unites us. Precisely, at the shoreline of our endeavors is where our minds are stimulated to solve the vexing equations of our organized concerns. Here, our spirits are quickened to meet the challenges of today, thus facilitating the promises of tomorrow.

Where each island ends and the mighty sea washes ashore, a miracle of transformation occurs. We call the essence of this miracle, inspiration and imagination, and the applied process of ingenuity toward productivity, we call discovery and invention.

We see in the frothy surf the collective energy of human ambition. It beckons us to embark on a voyage toward perfection. Then, as it gently caresses the sand of our various shores and retreats once again, we observe the vast potential of participating in the sharing of the sum of human knowledge and wisdom.

As each island of endeavor, whether an individual or group, taps into this source of light and truth, they expand the knowledge frontier. In so doing they enrich us all and contribute impetus to our ongoing voyage toward perfection.

The American Prophet, Joseph Smith, may have said it best when commenting on the writings of Saint Paul he wrote, "We believe in being honest, true, chaste, benevolent, virtuous, and in doing good to all men; indeed, we may say that we follow the admonition of Paul—we believe all things, we hope all things, we have endured many things, and hope to be able to endure all things. If there is anything virtuous, lovely, or of good report or praiseworthy, we seek after these things."

I have a dream-vision that new, independent producers of entertainment/communication projects in theatrical plays, films, television programming, special events, fairs, theme park designs and other interactive media, will arise with a renewed vision of and commitment to "Classic" family entertainment for the 21st century!

In my heart and mind's eye, I see a future where new creators of enriching entertainment such as that produced by George M. Cohen, Jerome Kern, Irving Berlin, Cole Porter, Richard Rogers, Oscar Hammerstein, Cecil B. DeMille, Frank Capra, Vincente Minnelli, Walt Disney and Louis B. Mayer of previous eras, will emerge anew.

It may take a decade or somewhat longer, but I envision it coming. Conversely, I can not conceive that the benighted, unredeeming, hollow entities that masquerade as entertainment today can long endure.

Mediocrity, let alone the current productions that represent the baser instincts of man, has no part in the redeeming spirit of the Lord that is calling to us to improve ourselves, to indeed embark on a voyage toward perfection.

It is directly on this fulcrum of enlightened entertainment, whose creators are inspired by the Light of Christ, that our future well being as healthy, viable families in a prosperous nation balances. Let us choose the better part, that which is virtuous. Let us support those who are creating new forms of inspirational entertainment. These new forms of optimistic communication and entertainment will become a transparent portal inviting all (youth and adults) to step through and discover the shape and hope of the positive things to come.

Errol Flynn:
A Man of Passion

Once upon a time in Hollywood, there was a young aspiring actor who had been discovered in 1934 England performing in repertory theater in Northampton. Soon thereafter, he was put under contract by Irving Asher, production head of Warner Brothers' Teddington Studios, near London. Asher, based on a hunch, promoted this neophyte actor to a starring role in *Murder at Monte Carlo*, his first film for Warner, and only his second film overall.

He arrived at Warner Bros. Burbank studios in early 1935 after appearing in two more unremarkable films in 1934 for Asher in England. Then came the break that launched one of the most remarkable movie careers in the history of Hollywood film production!

The plum role of Peter Blood that had been ticketed for the respected Robert Donat unexpectedly fell to the available and unknown Errol Flynn. This surprise turn of events occurred when Donat fell ill and last minute negotiations between Donat and the studio fell through. With *Captain Blood* nearly ready to go into production, Jack Warner and director Michael Curtiz needed a quick fix.

Warner recalled the telegram regarding Flynn and his contract that was sent to him by Asher in October, 1934. In part it read: "Signed today...best picture bet we have ever seen...excellent actor, champion boxer, swimmer-guarantee he's real find!"

The genuine qualities observed in Flynn by Asher of strong and athletic physical attributes, combined with charming personality and native intelligence, set him apart from many of his peers. In retrospect, he is even more unique from all but a few of the two generations of actors since.

What moviegoers saw when the movie palace lights were lowered and the silver screen flickered into life with the moving images of *Captain Blood*, was captivating. Flynn was an unpolished gem, but a gem nonetheless. The raw energy radiating from Flynn's first major performance was clear for anyone to see with a modicum of love for films.

A magic matrix of successful motion picture production elements began to emerge. The dazzling Flynn persona, with the refined charm of the lovely Olivia de Havilland, the quintessential protagonism of Basil Rathbone and many competent character actors, became the Flynn model at Warner Bros. for his many future productions.

In addition to being surrounded by competent actors, Flynn found his ideal stylistic auteur in action/adventure director Michael Curtiz. The other essential creative component was esteemed Austrian composer Erich Wolfgang Korngold who made his debut as a film composer with *Captain Blood*. Korngold's compositions and to a somewhat lesser degree, those of the prolific Max Steiner, became a recognizable creative signature of future Warner, Curtiz, Flynn collaborations.

However, the key component of any Flynn film was Flynn himself. Errol Flynn was a young virtuoso capable of projecting images of endearing sensitivity, soaring nobility, robust manliness and unflagging courage! Part of the reason for this unique ability, was that by the age of twenty or so, Flynn had already lived enough adventures for several life times.

At one time or another, he had worked as a cadet in training in government services in New Guinea, followed by a period working as an overseer on a copra plantation, to entering into a charter sailing partnership of a small schooner. Flynn followed this venture with a fling at gold mining and managing a tobacco plantation (both in New Guinea), to writing a column about life in that country for the *Sydney Bulletin*.

All of these varied experiences added something unique to the sum of Flynn's rapidly developing personality, intellectual awareness of peoples and situations, and of course, his dashing charm!

As I now reflect on many of the cultural influences of my youth that shaped my life's values and ideals, my recollections always come to rest on several factors. Prominent among those factors are the childhood reminiscences of viewing Flynn movies during the early years of television in the fifties in Los Angeles, California.

Many have commented on how disappointed Flynn was with the lack of respect and approbation toward his body of work by film critics, and others within the Academy of Motion Picture Arts and Sciences. Film critics often panned his performances as being devoid of emotional depth and texture. Many industry insiders thought Flynn's skills were one dimensional and lacking in scope.

I do not think film historians, critics or perhaps even Flynn himself, correctly comprehended the profound influence his films exerted on young people (especially boys) who often sought direction for their lives during that era. I for one will gladly testify that the heroic imagery of the majority of screen roles he portrayed made an indelible and positive impression on my adolescent psyche. They were always a constant source of encouragement for me to persevere toward achieving worthwhile goals, no matter what obstacles life might place in your path.

Flynn's pivotal role of Major Geoffrey Vickers in Warner's 1936 release of *The Charge of the Light Brigade* is an epic cinematic drama of valor and courage in the face of overwhelming opposition and near certain death. His moving performance in a story where his character neither wins the girl nor survives the conflict, is far closer to the zenith of such cinematic portrayals, than its nadir!

Flynn's seventh film for Warner Bros in Hollywood was indeed a memorable one. If ever there was one movie that fans associated with a certain star as his or her trademark film, it was *The Adventures of Robin Hood*. It was as if the gods of motion picture production construed to bring together all the cinematic elements essential to an actor's ideal performance and choreographed them into an archetype of near perfection. Only two other films come to mind in that regard—Clark Gable as Rhett Butler in *Gone with the Wind*; and Humphrey Bogart as Rick Blaine in *Casablanca*.

However, Flynn's *Hood* preceded Gable's *GWTW* by a year and Bogart's *Casablanca* by four years.

Errol Flynn the actor and Robin Hood, the fictional literary character, were nearly interchangeable, at least in the eyes of many of Flynn's growing legion of fans. In his portrayal of the legendary Saxon rogue hero of Sherwood Forrest who defies Norman tyranny, it wasn't so much an effort of acting the part as being it!

I'm not implying that Flynn did not possess competent acting skills; to the contrary, he was excellent. The point is this; all actors relied on past experiences for motivation and frame of reference to help them interpret their roles. It's just in Flynn's case, he was cast into stories where the central character was often confronted by situations and issues that required his character to search his soul deeply as to what was truth and inherently good as opposed to what was fallacy and ultimately evil.

Flynn, by his youthful enthusiasm and adventuresome experiences, his parents' love of culture and science, his own passion for independence and his regal baring, made him somewhat more natural in genuinely expressing the sentiments of classic idealism and nobility of purpose on the silver screen!

Executive producer, Hal B. Wallis, had assembled a topnotch production crew including director Curtiz, composer Korngold, screenwriters Norman Reilly Raine, and Seton I. Miller, art director Carl Weyle, costume designer Milos Anderson and makeup by Perc Westmore.

The large cast was excellent as well and featured former Flynn acting mates as Olivia de Havilland, Basil Rathbone, Claude Raines, Patrick Knowles, Montague Love and others.

Hence, all the pieces were assembled and ready to be put into place like some magical collage of artistic expression. What evolved after several months from this collaboration of Warner's finest talents was a landmark film that is still to this day, the quintessential example of the swashbuckler film genre. Hundreds of films have been produced in this genre and few of them compare to Warner's 1938 release of this masterpiece of pageantry, court intrigue, romance and rebellion.

No other film of this genre equals the sum total of its varied parts. Contemporary films appear pallid and nearly lifeless when viewed in comparison to the rich tapestries created within the artistic production of *The Adventures of Robin Hood*. It, like other great film classics of the era is a unique motion picture accomplishment.

Close your eyes for a moment and think of the last time you viewed this movie—what scenes come to mind? Perhaps the sunlight filtering through the leaves of Sherwood as Robin sought to explain his motives in protecting the defenseless, and providing shelter and food to the homeless to Maid Marion, is first among your recollections. Maybe, it is an early scene where Robin enters the castle of corrupt Sir Guy of Gisbourne where the Norman barons are having a feast in honor of Prince John while plotting to seize Richard the Lion Heart's kingdom.

You could select any number of scenes from this exquisite film and they would undeniably reflect the unique spirit, charm, romance and passion radiated by the film's leading man. At the center of everything in this film is the larger than life persona of Errol Flynn.

He endowed Robin Hood and indeed all of his roles with a profound believability! What greater attribute can an actor possess?

When an actor can so envelope the audience through his role portrayal, into identifying with the story and its characters, that they suspend incredulity for two hours and emotionally come vicariously to live the story through the moving images—That's acting!

Just like baseball's Willie Mays "The Say Hey Kid" could make phenomenal catches in the outfield for the New York Giants seem routine, so also, could Flynn make the difficult challenge of portraying idealistic characters dealing heroically with the evil opposition seem utterly genuine.

Mays' acrobatic plays were not routine for anyone, except for him, because of his extraordinary athletic gifts and passion for baseball.

In like fashion, Flynn's charismatic motion picture portrayals were not routine for anyone, except him, because of his rich and varied gifts, life experiences and his passionate spirit.

For your review and consideration, I have listed some of Flynn's best movies and the intriguing roles he animated on screen during his tumultuous life and flamboyant career:

Character Title Year Rating

1. Peter Blood *Captain Blood* 1935 4 stars
2. Maj. Geoffrey Vickers *Charge of the Light Brigade* 1936 4.75 stars
3. Robin Hood *The Adventures of Robin Hood* 1938 5 stars
4. Capt. Courtney *The Dawn Patrol* 1938 4.25 stars
5. Wade Hatton *Dodge City* 1939 4.50 stars
6. Earl of Essex *The Private Lives of Elizabeth and Essex* 1939 3.75 stars
7. Capt. Geoffrey Thorpe *The Sea Hawk* 1940 5 stars
8. Kerry Bradford *Virginia City* 1940 4.25 stars
9. Lt. Douglas Lee *Dive Bomber* 1941 3.75 stars
10. George A. Custer *They Died with Their Boots On* 1942 4.75 stars
11. James J. Corbett *Gentleman Jim* 1942 4.5 stars
12. Steve Wagner *Northern Pursuit* 1943 3.50 stars
13. Major Nelson *Objective Burma* 1945 5 stars
14. Clay Hardin *San Antonio* 1945 4.25 stars
15. Phil Gayley *Never Say Goodbye* 1946 3.75 stars
16. Don Juan de Marana *Adventures of Don Juan* 1949 4.75 stars
17. Soames Forsyte *That Forsyte Woman* 1949 3.5 stars
18. Brian Hawke *Against All Flags* 1952 3.75 stars
19. Jamie Durrisdeer *The Master of Ballantrae* 1953 4 stars

Summary: Errol Flynn with few exceptions was almost always cast as the heroic leading man in tales of adventure. Generally, he portrayed characters who courageously confronted the forces of tyranny. He imbued these roles with nobility of purpose, disarming wit, and unflagging resolve.

These were not reed thin characters; to the contrary, Flynn breathed the passion of life into them. They became real people up there on the screen who we wanted to believe in, to emulate and to cheer. If Flynn was only moderately talented, he could never have entertained and captivated the imaginations of millions for nearly two decades. No one is that good of an imposter to emotionally carry away audiences for two hours repeatedly over many years! People can discern real talent from play acting and emotional dishonesty.

I do not care what critics, historians or other stuffy highbrow types may have thought, said or written of him. The legions of Flynn fans worldwide were not concerned with the esoteric conversations at Hollywood cocktail parties regarding the relative acting merits of film stars.

Millions of average movie fans of the era felt they new him. They new Flynn was no saint, that he had personal flaws as did everyone. Maybe his were more magnified because of the larger than life existence he lived as a top Hollywood star. Yet, his fans adored him because something endearing in his essence of personality spoke to the everyman in each of us who sat in a darkened theater. It said, "Yes, you can achieve your goals in spite of your flaws if you just persevere and continue to believe in yourself and those around you." We believed!

The Uniquely American Spirit
of *Gone with the Wind*

Scarlett O'Hara, the central character in Margaret Mitchell's epic tale of the Old South during the Civil War, symbolizes the unflagging hope in the redemptive power of love and romantic ideals to deliver one from the chaos of war and its turbulent aftermath.

Gone with the Wind was most likely, the most popular novel of the twentieth century, and certainly the most eagerly awaited motion picture to be produced from a fictional novel.

When *Gone with the Wind* was translated to the silver screen through the cooperative efforts of Selznick International and MGM studios in 1939, nothing was spared in order to produce a landmark motion picture of grand proportions that would not disappoint the legions of readers of Ms Mitchell's best-selling novel.

From the beginning, it was assumed that the story's leading man could only be played by one actor—Hollywood's king, Clark Gable. The casting of Scarlett was much more challenging. After an exhaustive nationwide search, the film's producer and studio mogul, David O. Selznick, selected mercurial English actress Vivien Leigh to play Scarlett.

Hollywood's finest production talent was assembled to create *Gone with the Wind*. Victor Fleming came from MGM to direct the film just as he was completing directing principal photography on *The Wizard of Oz*. The memorable music score was composed by the incomparable Max Steiner and the impressive production design was by the highly respected William Cameron Menzies.

Epic entertainment always begins with a high concept and the written word. Numerous writers were employed by Selznick to bring Ms Mitchell's literary classic to the screen. Ultimately, after the efforts of several screen writers and many rewrites, veteran writer Sidney Howard received credit for the screenplay. Candidly, I believe Mr. Selznick who personally oversaw every aspect of production, had as much input to the final script as anyone.

Following Steiner's evocative overture and the film's credits, comes a brief but moving prolog that establishes the emotional as well as historical setting for the extraordinary motion picture experience to follow: "There was a land of Cavaliers and Cotton Fields called the Old South…Here in this pretty world gallantry took its last bow…Here was the last ever to be seen of Knights and their Ladies Fair, of Master and of Slave…Look for it only in books, for it is no more than a dream remembered. A Civilization gone with the wind…"

If a few passages could convey the essence of a 1037 page novel, then perhaps consider excerpts of the author's prose from the last two pages:

"Scarlett, when you are forty-five, perhaps you will know what I am talking about, and then perhaps you, too, will be tired of imitation gentry and shoddy manners and cheap emotions. But I doubt it. I think you'll always be more attracted by glister than by gold. Anyway, I can't wait that long to see. And I have no desire to wait. It just doesn't interest me…Well, you get my meaning, don't you?"

"No," she cried. "All I know is that you do not love me and you are going away! Oh, my darling, if you go what shall I do?"

"I'm too old to shoulder the burden of constant lies that go with living in polite disillusionment. I couldn't live with you and lie to you, and I certainly couldn't lie to myself. I can't even lie to you now. I wish I could care what you do or where you go, but I can't…My dear, I don't give a damn."

She knew now that he had meant every word he said…she knew because she sensed in him something strong, unyielding, implacable—all the qualities she had looked for in Ashley and never found. She had never understood either of the men she had loved, and so she had lost them both. Now, she had a fumbling knowledge that, had she ever understood Ashley, she would have never have loved him; had she ever understood Rhett, she would never have lost him. She wondered forlornly if she had ever really understood anyone in the world. "I won't think of it now," she thought grimly, summoning up her old charm. "I'll go crazy if I think about losing him now. I'll think of it tomorrow."

She had gone back to Tara once in fear and defeat, and she had emerged from its sheltering walls strong and armed for victory…With the spirit of her people who would not know defeat, even when it stared them in the face, she raised her chin. She could get Rhett back. She knew she could…"I'll think of it all tomorrow, at Tara. I can stand it then…"

"Tomorrow, I'll think of some way to get him back. After all, tomorrow is another day."

Strong-willed people must never lose faith in the promise of the future. No matter what calamitous events our personal or societal follies have caused us to endure, our Judeo-Christian ethic holds out the promise of a better tomorrow. The deliverance from evil is at once both temporal and spiritual.

In times past, it was referred to as the "Hope of Israel," meaning that the twelve tribes descendant from the ancient patriarch, Jacob, would not lose sight of, or faith in, the prophetic promise made to them anciently. As contained in holy writ, the promise is that Israel will ultimately occupy the Holy Lands in peace and prosperity, free to worship Jehovah (Jesus Christ), the God of Israel.

Americans, by nature, seem to have inbred into their souls at birth this essential optimism. It is our birthright, bequeathed to us by our pilgrim forefathers and vouchsafed by the founding fathers in liberty. Our cultural heritage bequeaths to us the richest of treasures—faith in tomorrow. At the core of this faith is the immutable testimony of the Holy Spirit that Jesus is the Christ, the Son of God! However soft the voice of spirit is, it resides in most citizens who are native to this blessed land of promise or immigrated to it legally. It only awaits our earnest appeal whenever harrowing times threaten our tranquility, our sovereignty, or our very lives. It has the power to transform us from quaking, forlorn individuals into a courageous people of resolve, not content to accept defeat or mediocrity in any of its myriad manifestations.

In its purest form, this American faith in the future and love of the land is the underlying thematic spirit that permeates *Gone with the Wind*. It is this hopefulness regarding the future that has sustained Americans from the beginning in the War of Independence through the Great Depression and two World Wars. It is this basic American spirit of goodness, faith, virtue of character, loyalty to timeless ideals and values, and nobility of purpose, that is sadly missing from nearly all modern entertainment.

If you have not viewed recently such faith promoting classics as *The Robe*, *Quo Vadis*, *The Ten Commandments*, *King of Kings*, *The Greatest Story Ever Told*, *Miracle of the Bells*, or *Ben Hur*, take time to do so. You will experience the true joy of epic and faith promoting film making.

With the passing of the Studio System era in the late fifties, it wasn't long till the death knell also sounded for classic motion pictures which represented great family entertainment and incorporated the timeless values and noble ideals of Western civilization and traditions. As Margaret Mitchell wrote, it was, "A civilization gone with the wind."

Heavenly Strains, Cosmology and Spirit Matter

The Last Full Measure of Devotion

No earthly king or potentate,
rules beyond a certain date,
which are the natural boundaries,
of their second estate.

The important thing in life
is not the number of days
one spends in mortality,
rather, the quality of our lives
in serving the needs of others.

Some seek only
to satiate the hungering ends
of their own self-serving individual estate,
without ever a thought or good Samaritan's deed
to the benefit of others.

They hearken unto the spirit of Lucifer,
he who led a third of the host of Heaven astray
and now is called the devil—
he who tempts the children of men…
to lust after carnal things,
power and dominion,
to lie, deceive and kill.
Oh, these shall never know
the diverse and resplendent joys of Heaven.

Then,
there is a second group,
who would not stoop to such vile behavior.
Yet, neither do they attempt
to ascend to the heights of excellence,
content to rest upon the fence
of non-striving mediocrity.

These lukewarm terrestrial souls
make up the greater part of humanity.
Afraid of the consequences of leadership or failure
they spend their moderate days
in ordinary pursuits mending tremulous fences,
upon which they often perch—
content to enjoy non-taxing pleasantries.

This is not to say
they are not good,
for they surely are not bad.
They have simply lost their way
and no longer envision the grandeur of the Maker.
That motivating spark of divinity within us,
that compels us to take the road less traveled
and move beyond complacency,
is no longer found within them.

Now behold the celestial tier,
those who seldom failed
to think of others,
that turned not away
from the pleas for mercy,
or cries of help for sustenance.
These noble souls who strove to grasp
the cherished, golden ring of excellence,
to achieve something worthy of praise,
not merely to stroke their egos
rather, to enrich the lives of countless others.

These are they
who resist the enticements of the devil,
who are not swayed from the paths of righteousness
by the siren calls of fame or fortune...

These are they
who strive mightily
to turn faults into strengths,
to improve upon their talents,
to create pleasing works of beauty…
inspiring us to comprehend the mind of God.
Thus, by sharing their refining gift
they empower and lift the broken spirits of others.

These are they
who sometimes fall short,
but in lieu of giving up,
strive anew to win the race of life.
No matter how often they fall,
they pick themselves up and stumble on
toward the distant finish line.
They might not win, show or place,
but in the end it simply doesn't matter.
For they who run the race to the end
have already won the garland of victory—
having overcome the trial of adversity,
that those who shrink in the shadows
of mediocrity's superficial security,
will never know.

Lastly, these are they
who freely give of their time
to serve greater purposes than themselves.
They answer the call of nobility,
to oppose the forces of darkness
and the perils threatened by ruthless despots
and terrorists brimming with hate.
They resist the common urge to flee

and courageously place themselves in the path
of the calamitous tendencies of murdering tyrants
who mindlessly recite "God is great,"
yet know him not, nor his charity he so readily proffers
to Jew, Arab and Gentile.

These are they
who give as Abraham Lincoln said,
"the last full measure of devotion,"
selflessly laying down their lives if so called upon,
as a testament of faith upon the alter of God,
in order to preserve for ourselves
as well as other peace loving souls of all nations,
the priceless fruits of Heavenly ordained liberty!

A Shooting Star

A shooting star
behaves as though
a pompous flare,
a harbinger of great things to come.

Behold,
it expends itself
in gratuitous glory,
matter to light in ostentatious flight.

Why,
oh beauteous orb,
thou rock of interstellar space,
why cast thy might in futile flight
to outshine the starry night
and bounteous gems of heaven?

Oh,
flaming cinder,
preserve thy celestial essence,
thy comely shape divine.
Break free the yoke of gravity,
while a molecule of thy matter remaineth.

Hail,
and farewell to thee,
oh falling star.
Thou that plummets to earth
rapidly, so existentially,
then burns out and is no more.

And,
like a magic slate,
leaves only an imaginary trace
upon the mind,
Of what once was promethean
in human kind.

The Solution for a Tiny Blue Planet

We live on a tiny blue planet
just a speck of dust
really,
amidst all the glory of
infinite,
majestic creation.

We are quarantined
by intergalactic space
and by wisdom of the creator's grace
to live out our existence alone
in this solar system,
residing in the Milky Way Galaxy,
far, far away
from our Father, our Lord,
and innumerable family of man.
They've already passed this temporal way
and now eternally dwell
with them upon
Celestial spheres of light
nigh unto Kolob.

With our most powerful telescopes
we fail to pierce
the heavenly veil
and can not see them.
Thus we must proceed along
life's stardust trail on faith alone,
believing that Father and Son
know our travails and deeply care.

Here we dwell
on this tiny blue planet
in the fullness of time—
beset by a host of perplexing problems,
not the least of which are—war, terror, disease,
famine, global pollution, and nuclear expansion.

We've turned everywhere
seeking solutions—
to our governments, our wise scientists,
even to enlightened multi-national organizations,
but much to our chagrin
every order, level and body of government
at home and abroad,
appears to be rotting from within—
because of human greed and corruption.

The greatest plague of all—
far more threatening to our universal welfare
than cancer, insidious microbes,
some unknown strain of deadly virus or a chemist's nightmare,
is man's proclivity
to turn his back on God
in favor of humanism, existentialism and hedonistic carnality,
preferring to enjoy the unfulfilling wages of sin in lieu of
the ennobling Light of Christ.

If only man would kneel
and momentarily turn his soul in humble,
prayerful thoughts toward Heaven,
the coming disasters of war, plagues and famine
could yet be averted—

if only man would hearken to the prophets,
cease his insane folly, shun idolatry
and embrace the life giving properties
of virtue and righteousness—
the approaching calamities might well be avoided.

These proverbs of wisdom and only these,
contain the proverbial seeds of principled solutions
for peoples in turmoil and nations conflicted,
on this endangered temporal orb wanting in viable solutions—
this tiny blue planet.

Dedication to Dreamers

To all the dreamers everywhere,
and of every era,
no matter the time nor the place,
I dedicate my thoughts to you.

For those who take the time
to dream,
and then follow through
are truly heroes.

No matter the dimensions
grandiose or small,
all dreams reflect an inner light
that strives to prevail against the dark night of conformity,
to overcome the balky, rigid, infertile minds
and the darkness of perverted souls
and their binding tyranny of erroneous notions.

The first of all dreamers
was called the Word,
and the Word was the light of truth;
and the darkness failed to comprehend
that the Word was the Son of God
who moved upon the unorganized void.

Thus, as the archetype of creators,
created he the heavens and then the earth,
as a lovely temporal abode upon which
all of Father's spirit children could dwell.

We come from our heavenly home
to abide on earth,
clothed in flesh and bone
to see if we will live righteously,
and follow him who said:
"I am the way and the life,
he who follows me…"
shall live eternally.

Many dreamers have come
and gone since then.
All have enriched our lives in some meaningful way
or surely could,
if we would only open our hearts and minds
and let them light the way.

Look down the corridors of time
and pray tell me what do you see?
Why of course you see,
men of passion striving to be free,
free to create liberating objects
of beauty, grace and nobility.

This tribute goes out to men
like Joseph of Palestine,
who dreamed of his future destiny
in ancient times in the lands of Pharaoh
and miraculously saved his family and Egypt
from the ravages of drought and famine.

Since that ancient time till now,
countless souls have passed
across the varied scenes of life…
but few have left an enduring mark

as the dreamers who envision new ways of discovery,
who design and create—
as Marco Polo, Columbus, Leonardo, and Michelangelo;
as Shakespeare, Milton, Bach, Mozart and Handel;
as Gutenberg, Copernicus, Galileo, Franklin, and Tesla.
Wondrous works of adventure, science and art did they create;
and enriched our lives forevermore with their poetry and prose,
paintings and sculpture, music and lyrics,
discoveries and inventions.

Oh, the majesty
of imaginative people,
they reflect the light of the creative,
divine, omniscient mind.

Something's in the Air

I was sitting there
uneasy in my favorite chair,
troubled by the evening news
and contemplating days of tenuous life ahead,
when…
a silent voice
whispered in my ear—
"Something's in the air."

I looked around
for the source of the words spoken to me,
but, I was alone in the room—
when again…
came the permeating refrain
to my inner ear and registering
on my psyche—
"Something's in the air."

It sends a chill up and down
the length of me,
not knowing what it is,
yet,
I feel it lingering near to me…
what does it portend—good or evil—
some specter to loath and fear
or embrace effulgently?

And so I spoke aloud
in tremulous speech to the incorporeal voice,
"Tell me oh specter's voice,
what portend these words to me?"

And the still small voice unhesitatingly rejoined,
"Look all around your world
and what do you see?"
Thus, the specter questioned me.

"I see much that dampens my spirit."
I forthrightly answered,
"children abused, murders in diverse places,
corruption in high stations, terrorist acts of violence,
nuclear proliferation and tension between nations…
that is what I see…
and it brings much sadness."

I listened for the invisible spirit's answer,
however, there was only silence—
except for the rapid beating of my heart,
nothing was said for what seemed an hour
yet, was only peaceful moments.
Then once more,
came the message of the deep permeating voice—
"Do not give in to despair."

Again I swiveled my head
peering about the room,
but, I was still alone…
then, even deeper within I heard,
"There is a light that shines
amidst all this gloom and darkness—
a light of truth that points the way
to eternal peace and happiness."

"Oh, goodly spirit," I inquired,
"is that what I feel,
that something in the air—
is that the light that shines in darkness?"

"That depends on you."
answered the ethereal voice.
"Are you a man of faith, virtue and goodwill to others…
or are you shallow, lustful, and negative—
a cynic toward all spiritual things?"

"If you are the former,
you will perceive the light
that shines amidst the darkness
and be drawn unto it,
you will embrace the light fully,
and be filled with this warming light within—
illuminating yourself and those whom you love…
this life giving light of truth and virtue
will show the pathway to everlasting joy
and family exaltation!"

"However, if you are the latter,
you will fail to perceive the light
and will continue on as you were before…
lost in the obscure darkness of earthly cares,
unable to escape the endless void of sightless night—
entirely devoid of truth or light."

I was shivering with fright
after hearing this painful proclamation.
While I hoped I was the former,
most likely, I would fall into the latter
classification of wayward, disobedient men—
could there be some hope for me?

While I yet ruminated
on this question,
the unseen spirit's words returned to me…

"Do not fear,
there is a way prepared
for all the likes of you…
for you who desire to do good,
to be obedient—but at times
have strayed from the straight path of truth and light
and have sinned—
the Father knows the righteous desires of your heart,
and unto you extends his mercy…
through his redemptive plan."

My heart and soul
yearned to hear more
of this soothing balm for tormented minds
that proffered saving grace
and I exclaimed, "Goodly spirit,
stop not till you share it all with me."

The spirit inquired,
"Do you read the Holy Bible?"
"Yes, occasionally," I stammered—
"however, so many read it differently
among the various churches—
its true meaning isn't always clear to me."

"It is for this very purpose
the Father has raised up an American prophet
of the latter days,
and through him published to the world
a companion book of scripture—
that testifies of his Son in plain and simple words,
so that all who humble themselves before him
might know the truth.

This sacred scripture bares solemn testimony
that the Son is the Light of Truth of which all the
holy prophets spoke and bore record,
that the Lamb of God must come into the world
and be put to death,
that he might become an infinite ransom
for all the sins of man,
that he might draw all men unto him,
and raise them up unto life everlasting…
that as he was raised upon the cross
for all to see,
and gave his life willingly—
that all men might cleanse themselves
of their sins through his precious blood
and repent of their carnal natures while in the flesh—
and come forth out of the waters of baptism
a new creation of the spirit,
unto eternal life…
and every knee shall bow
and every tongue confess
that he is the King of Kings, the Alpha and Omega,
the Lord of Hosts, the Prince of Peace,
the Glorified Resurrected Savior,
the living Son of God—this child of Bethlehem, who grew
from grace to grace to virtuous manhood—
this Jesus of Nazareth, known as a carpenter's son,
who learned obedience by the things he suffered,
until finally, in the Garden of Gethsemane
he descended beneath all things and suffered all
to the point of pain and anguish, that he bled from every pore…
and thus following his death on Calvary
and coming forth on the third day from the tomb—
he stood forth triumphant over death and the grave—
the First Fruit of the Resurrection,
He was, is and shall eternally be—Jesus The Christ!"

By this time I had slumped to the floor
with tears streaming down my face,
I pleaded once more,
"Where is this sacred record of the divinity of Jesus,
how may I acquire it to read for myself and likewise be edified..."

"Look," the spirit calmly said,
and I raised my tear stained face
to the end table next to my chair,
and resting there was a leather bound book
with the title embossed in gold—
The Book of Mormon.

"This is the Father's gift to you,
and to all those who seek the truth in humility,
for none but the sincere and humble seekers of truth
can understand and receive these plain and simple truths
of the gospel of Jesus Christ,
and only those who read the contents of these pages prayerfully,
may receive a witness of its truth as have you."

"But, Holy Spirit, I have not read the book as yet—
it is true that I have been offering a silent prayer in my heart
for many weeks to understand the calamity of our earth
and to know the meaning of life...how is it that I have been so
blessed?"

"The Father who knows the thoughts of all men's hearts,
knew you would accept the book with unbounded joy
when given a chance—here is your opportunity—
embrace the truths of this marvelous work and wonder
to your bosom and when your testimony is strengthened,
share your witness with others."

"Now, I must take my leave of you so I might testify to others...
live faithfully and you will have the peace of Jesus Christ
in your heart till the end of your earthly days,
no matter what troubles occur in the world—
always remember tonight—
for Truth and Light are in the air!"

With that, I felt a heavenly presence leave my room—
but of this I am sure, as long as I read this book prayerfully
and follow its principles—I shall never be troubled of mind
or spirit again as I had been before...
nor, shall I ever feel alone!

I'm Coming Back to Thee

(an anthem of hope for all who may have
strayed and temporarily lost their way)

Oh my Lord,
I'm coming back,
I'm coming back to thee
to fulfill my mission
in service to my fellow man.
Yea, to add my part
in my own individual way
to build thy kingdom
while awaiting thee.

Oh my Lord,
I'm coming back,
I'm coming back to thee
by thy mercy, grace
and ever open helping hand.
Yea, my heart does ache
for having strayed at times
in distant fields of play
far, far away from thee.

Oh my Lord,
I'm coming back,
I'm coming back to thee
to live out my destiny
in a manner pleasing thee.
Yea, how my broken
contrite spirit does plead my case
in humble prayer and on bended knee,
open thy door a second time
to this retched beggar-waif
and drive not this pitiful soul away from thee.

Oh my Lord,
I'm coming back,
I'm coming back to thee
animated by thy gracious
life-giving spirit wiser than before.
Yea, committed to thy straight path
and the virtue of obedience,
my soul in joyous righteousness
sings out evermore to thee,
this anthem for sinners repented—
for thou does also love the prodigal son,
and nothing can delay or deter me more.

Oh my Lord,
in this blessed thing
my grateful heart does rejoice
and declares for angels and men to hear,
I'm coming back,
I'm coming back to thee!

Oh, Celebrate the Joys
(Of Our Eternal Lord)

1. His strength is never lacking, in supporting us when weary;

2. His hand is always open, grasping ours in loving brotherhood;

3. His ears are always listening, to every cry of pain or whisper of regret.

Oh, celebrate the joys, and contemplate the holy babe illuminated in a manger, beneath the star of Bethlehem!

4. His compassion never falters, when sins beget us sorrows;

5. His grace will carry us, when we try to come unto him, no matter how oft we stumble or even if we fall;

6. His mercy is granted to all who exercise faith unto repentance and cultivate virtue and righteousness in every deed and thought.

Oh, celebrate the joys, the infinite bounties of his wondrous, eternal grace!

7. He's always there for us, though countless times we've strayed;

8. He encompasses the broken heart and contrite spirit, with unconditioned love;

9. He embodies truth and light, a fount of flowing wisdom unto all who thirst for truth to live more abundantly the humble, faithful life.

Oh, celebrate the joys, of soothing balm to hurtful hearts and troubled minds of unimagined peace!

10. He at Gethsemane, suffered the will of the Father and drank the bitter cup and took upon himself the sins of all mankind;

11. He paid the price of broken law, a spotless sacrificial lamb, as only he, the Son of God, in perfect righteousness could do;

12. He at Calvary, finished his temporal work his Father had anointed him to do, as he hung upon the cross in agony and uttered, "Forgive them, Father, for they know not what they do."

Oh, celebrate the joys, of he who willingly gave his life and took it up once more!

13. He is the living Savior, who organized the heavens and appointed the heavenly orbs their times and seasons; He is the power which sustains them and the source of light that illuminates the stars, the sun and moon, and yes, even the earth upon which we stand, he is also the light that shines to give us sight and quickens the mind of man, that eternal truths we might providentially comprehend;

14. He is the living Savior, who fulfilled the ancient prophets, recompensed the law, fed the hungry, healed the sick, raised the dead, walked upon the water; and preached his everlasting gospel while yet he sojourned among the people and gathered he his sheep, that heard his voice and were numbered among his humble flock;

15. He is the living Savior, who rescues us from Adam's fall, triumphs over death, the grave, and ransoms us from Satan's lair, that we not be denied the everlasting joys of Heaven;

16. He is the living Savior, of whom the angel in the empty sepulcher declared unto Mary, "Why seek ye the living among the dead?" And again, the greatest proclamation ever made, "He is not here: for he is risen."

Oh, celebrate the joys of he whom in the beginning was the word of truth and light of Heaven!

17. He is the living Savior, of whom testifies the seraphic hosts, the scriptures, the prophets, and the quiet, whispering voice of Holy Ghost—he was in the beginning with the Father, he was Jehovah who spoke to Moses from a burning bush, he was Jesus the carpenter's son, who laid down his life and took it up again;

18. He is the living Savior, who revealed himself to prophets in olden days as diverse as Noah, Abraham, Jacob, Joseph and Moses, and gave them laws and commandments by which in faithful righteousness they were meant to live and worship the Only Begotten of the Father;

19. He is the living Savior, who in the meridian of time, was the child of sacred birth in Bethlehem, unto whom three wise men came bearing gifts from afar, and established he his earthly kingdom as he walked and taught his gospel in old Jerusalem;

20. He is the living Savior, of whom the Father said — "This is my beloved Son, hear him" — as he spoke to a young boy full of faith, to usher in this final dispensation of the fullness of times upon a waiting earth;

21. He is the living Savior, who after long dark centuries of apostasy, again appeared to man on earth — even to Joseph Smith in latter days to restore his kingdom anew; to prepare a New Jerusalem, unto which will flow all who desire to worship him in truth and righteousness; as also will come the lost tribes of ancient Israel and assuredly assist the saints to build a glorious temple to the Most High where they will receive their Redeemer and usher in a millennium of perfect peace and infinite glory too.

Oh, celebrate the joys, for the time soon approaches, when every knee will bow, and every tongue confess…

He is the living Savior, the Son of God — this Jesus of Nazareth, he is the King of Kings, the Prince of Peace, the anointed one…for Jew, Gentile and Saint.

Oh, celebrate the joys of his abundant gifts to us of renewal and radiant celestial life, where fathers, mothers and children are bound together by his effulgent love — one glorious eternal family to rule and reign with the Only Begotten of the Father — the risen, glorious…eternal living Christ!

Christmas in America

Celebrating Christmas in Metropolis or Small Town

This is a special time of year when store windows, main streets and shopping malls are gaily festooned with the lights and symbols of Christmas. Children line up to sit on Santa's knee and share a Christmas wish. In many company offices, employees gather to share a cup of hot cider, exchange gifts, and wish each other the joys of the season before departing for the holidays.

Everywhere we go and nearly everyone we meet, seems to have a glowing countenance and more personal warmth than normal, if only for a fleeting time. People seem to be more willing than usual to help one another—even strangers. In general, there appears to be greater patience, forbearance, forgiveness, thoughtfulness, charity, peace and goodwill toward our fellow man, than at any other time or season of the year.

In communities just like yours annual Christmas parades are often held. The most famous is the historic Macy's spectacular in Manhattan, NY, that is broadcast nationwide on live television. One of the most popular attractions of this enduring Yule holiday event, are giant, colorful, inflatable character figures. You might see any number of comic heroes from Mickey Mouse, to Bugs Bunny or even a super hero or two. Each of these enormously large helium filled characters is held securely by thirty or so marching volunteers.

One by one, the gargantuan blimps in the forms of animals, mascots and comic heroes slowly make their way down the parade route intermingled with marching bands, Broadway cast show performers, the Music City Rockettes, and others. Last to appear, is Santa in his sleigh, pulled by twelve flying reindeer, as all pass in review of thousands of excitable fans lining the boulevard.

Lest we forget, small town America is equally dedicated to producing colorful events that reflect their unique spirit and setting. The traditional small town parade is a staple of the heartland. I live in such a community. West Branch, Iowa, is the birthplace of President Herbert Hoover and his presidential library and museum are located here. Annually, our town stages special events that ooze the essence of Americana.

A typical Christmas parade in a small Iowa Midwestern farm town might feature the mayor in an antique car leading a spirited procession down their historic main street. Following his honor, would come the local high school marching band, tooting their trombones, and playing other instruments for all they're worth, thus preserving the Hawkeye spirit of Meredith Wilson.

The band is usually followed by a half dozen festive floats built on flatbed trucks and sponsored by local merchants. Broadway it isn't, but the fun is in participating. Many in these strong communities volunteer to design, construct, paint or in some way contribute to the production of one or another of the colorful and locally sponsored floats.

Now comes the highlight of this prideful day. An old farmer's wooden hay wagon pulled by four chestnut horses and brightly draped in Christmas lights, red and green crepe, shiny tinsel and carrying bales of hay, features twelve spirited carolers and guess who? That's right, each year it's fun to try and guess which of several prominent local folk has been selected to play the man of the hour—old St. Nick.

Whomever it may be inside the bulky red costume and long white beard, from the HS football coach to the local postmaster, Santa vigorously waves, and reaching into a large cloth bag, retrieves small candies and throws them to the many admiring children lining the old main street. It's a wonderful heartland tradition!

It doesn't matter how sophisticated or un, big city or small, it's all fun, each on its own respective level.

Across the nation, many homes are preparing for the annual family celebration of the holidays. Relatives and friends you haven't seen since this time last year, are about to arrive bearing gifts and an appetite. Kitchens and dining rooms are filled with the aroma of freshly baked turkeys, chickens, and roasts. Additionally, the dining table is nearly overflowing with colorful side dishes of vegetables, fruits, real mashed potatoes and candied yams. Just waiting for a space to be cleared after the main course is finished, are tasty desserts homemade from grandma's tattered 1950 Betty Crocker Cookbook.

It's always a treat when mom lets the children participate in decorating the six-inch gingerbread cookies in the forms of Mr. and Mrs. Claus, reindeer, Christmas bells, toy soldiers, and snowmen! Then mom can assist the children in wrapping each one in red or green cellophane and attaching a name card for each of the invited guests. When completed, all the wrapped cookies are placed in a large basket decorated with holly and placed on a table in the entryway. That way as guests arrive, you can usher them into the spirit of the occasion by inviting them to find their personalized Christmas cookie and nametag.

Living rooms and dens carry their own distinct potpourri of delightfully mixed scents of pine cones, freshly cut and decorated trees, cinnamon scented candles, and strings of cranberries and popcorn strung on the tree. Top it all off with your own selection of Christmas music and you have quite a warm and inviting home environment in which you may enjoy family and friends.

One way to surely find the Christmas spirit of "Peace on Earth and Goodwill to Men," is to set aside some time for your family, neighborhood friends, church groups, fraternal organizations or any others to visit hospitals, nursing homes or hospices to spread hope and cheer to those that are ill and afflicted in body, mind or spirit, that may be in need in any of a hundred ways.

Spend some time on your knees in humble prayer to our Father in Heaven. Ask him in the name of his son, Jesus Christ, to inspire you with ideas as to how you may best serve the needy and less fortunate in your community.

Remember the charitable example of the Good Samaritan in the New Testament and leave your judgments of others and their predicaments behind. Your only question to yourself should be, how can I be of service to this individual or family? Perhaps you have more temporal resources at your disposal than is necessary for you personally or your family's needs. If so, I'm sure you'll find an appropriate way to assist your brother and his family.

Sometimes, all a person needs is someone to befriend them, to give a listening ear, or a sympathetic shoulder to lean on. Maybe they could use the benefit of a key introduction to an executive you know that does the hiring in a field of their interest. The spirit will guide you as you humble yourself before God and seek his council.

After all, it is indeed his birth that we are celebrating. It is his pervading spirit and omnipotent grace that reaches out to us during this special season with powerful balm to heal all manner of heartache and misery. All we need do is open our hearts and minds to him. When Jesus Christ knocks at any time of year, open the door and invite him in. You will be eternally grateful you did.

Lightning Source UK Ltd.
Milton Keynes UK
UKOW052003040112

184764UK00001B/50/P